From Foreign Child to Illegal Immigrant

The Case of T, a Brazilian Man of Japanese Descent Who Lived in Japan for 20 Years

Matsuo Tamaki

About the author

Matsuo Tamaki is a professor at the School of International Studies, Utsunomiya University. He is a representative of HANDS Project (it provides educational support for foreign students) which has been run by the Center for the Multicultural Public Sphere of the university. He holds a Ph.D. in Sociology. His main research themes are the issues of homelessness in Japan, international migration in East Asia and education for foreign students. Also, he is going to open a jishu yakan chugaku (volunteer nighttime junior high school) in Utsunomiya, Tochigi Prefecture from September, 2021. This school is mainly for the people who were not able to get compulsory education sufficiently and foreigners who want to learn Japanese language.

Utsunomiya University international studies library Vol.12

From Foreign Child to Illegal Immigrant
The Case of T, a Brazilian Man of Japanese Descent
Who Lived in Japan for 20 Years

Published by Matsuo Tamaki
Shimotsuke Shimbunsha
1-8-11 Showa, Utsunomiya-shi, Tochigi 320-8686, Japan

First English edition: August 2021

This book is a translation of
Aru gaikokujin no nihon deno 20nen -Gaikokujin jidouseito kara 'fuhoutaizaisya' e(THE SHIMOTSUKE NEWSPAPERS CO., LTD. 2019)

This work was supported by JSPS KAKENHI Grant Number 19H00604.
Printed by SHINANO PUBLISHING PRESS CO., LTD.
Book design by Takeshi Hashimoto, Design GEM

Printed in Japan
ISBN 978-4-88286-796-8
https://www.shimotsuke.co.jp/

To Futa, Sen, Rina, Ayana
and Katsuko

Foreword

Illegal residence refers to staying in a country where one does not possess citizenship and the required permission for residence. Illegal residents may be roughly divided into illegal overstayers, who have remained in the country beyond the time allotted to them, and illegal entrants, who have entered the country without permission. Both are subject to deportation. Most illegal residents in Japan are illegal overstayers; as of July 31, 2019, there were 79,013 such individuals in Japan. The long-term detention in immigration control facilities of illegal overstayers in Japan is currently considered a serious problem. In general, detention in immigration control facilities for six months or more is treated as long-term. According to the Ministry of Justice (MOJ), long-term detainees constituted approximately 50% of all detainees in Fiscal Year (FY) 2018.

The numbers of school-age children of foreign nationality (henceforth foreign children) have risen in Japan. The government has adopted a policy that compulsory education does not apply to foreign children; however, they may enroll in school if they choose to. Most of them are enrolled in Japanese public schools. As of May 1, 2018, of the 93,133 foreign students in public schools nationwide, 40,485 required Japanese language support (43.5% of the whole). Some 80% of these were native speakers of Portuguese, Chinese, Filipino, or Spanish (Ministry of Education, Culture, Sports, Science and Technology (MEXT), 2018). Their concerns include lack of understanding of Japanese, inability to follow lessons, inability to make friends, and being subject to bully attacks, thereby resulting in school non-attendance and low high school matriculation rates.

T is a Brazilian of Japanese descent who came to Japan in 1998 at the age of 10 years. He stopped attending school shortly after entering junior high school, and thereafter, he was involved in a repeated pattern of delinquency and crime. While in prison, he lost his status of residence as a long-term resident and became an illegal overstayer. Appealing against the deportation order, he sued the authorities but lost the case. After spending about three years in an MOJ Immigration Control Bureau detention center, he was deported to his home country of Brazil in November 2019. He was aged 31 years at the time.

This book follows T through his twenty years in Japan, as a translation of *A Foreigner's Twenty Years in Japan: From Foreign Child to Illegal Overstayer*, published in October 2019 by Shimotsuke Shimbunsha. T was deported to Brazil less than a month after the book was published. His family (parents and younger brother), who remain in Japan, have effectively been cut off from him, as—having been deported—he is essentially unable to return to Japan. I was able to communicate with T through Messenger just once after his return to Brazil, in March 2020; in response to multiple messages, he replied briefly “Yes, it's me. I'm okay and I'm doing my best, but I haven't found a job yet. Tell everyone I said hello.” According to T's mother, who spoke with him a few times by phone after his return, he seems to be homeless and eking out a living as a vendor.

A new year's card arrived from T in January 2020: "Dear Mr. Matsuo Tamaki, Happy New Year. I wish you and your family a very good 2020. I am used to being back in Brazil by now and am doing fine. Don't worry about me. From T." T had planned before his deportation for the card to arrive on time for the new year. The words "I am used to being back in Brazil by now and am doing fine. Don't worry about me" give the reader a sense of his kindness.

I was able to present T with a copy of *A Foreigner's Twenty Years in Japan* before his deportation, when I had no idea that he would be deported so soon. The publication of the book was simply one point along the way, and I was hoping to continue providing any support possible. Nothing about this has changed, even with T unreachable in faraway Brazil. My greatest hope is simply that he will survive. I hope to meet him one day in Brazil and talk about everything directly face to face, instead of through the acrylic divider of the detention center visitation room.

T says that he enjoyed life as an elementary school student; what, then, drove him away from school and into delinquency and crime once he began junior high school? What kept him from reform? To what extent should the fact of his delinquency and crime constrain his life? This book focuses on T as an individual to closely examine his twenty years in Japan.

The original text has been edited to some extent for

translation. The References section has likewise been edited to some extent. I very much hope that this book will be interesting for T.

本書に寄せて

不法滞在とは、自らが国籍を有する以外の国に在留許可が無い状態で滞在していることを指す。不法滞在者は滞在許可期間を超えて滞在する不法残留者と入国許可を受けていない不法入国者に大別される。いずれも、国外への退去強制の対象者となる。日本では、不法滞在者の大半は不法残留者である。2019年7月31日現在、日本には、7万9,013人の不法残留者がいる。現在、日本では不法滞在者の入管施設における長期収容が大きく問題視されている。一般に、入管施設における6か月以上の収容は長期収容と捉えられる。法務省によると、全被収容者に占める長期収容者の割合は、2018年度で約5割を占めている。

外国籍の児童生徒(以下、外国人児童生徒)が増えている。政府は,外国人児童生徒に就学義務を課しておらず、希望があれば入学を認めるという方針を採っている。外国人児童生徒の大半は日本の公立学校に在籍していると思われる。2018年5月1日現在、全国の公立学校に在籍している外国人児童生徒数は93,133人で、そのうち、日本語指導が必要な外国人児童生徒数は40,485人で、全体の43.5%を占める。日本語指導が必要な児童生徒の主要母語別状況は、ポルトガル語、中国語、フィリピノ語、スペイン語の4言語で全体の約8割を占める(文部科学省、2018年)。かれらは、日本語がわからない、勉強についていけない、友達ができない、いじめにあう等,様々な問題に直面している。それらは,不登校や低い高校進学率という問題につながる。

日系ブラジル人の児童として1998年に10歳の時に来日した男性のTは、中学校入学後間もなく不登校になり、その後,非行と犯罪を繰り返す。刑務所服役中に定住者の在留資格を失い、不法残留となる。退去強制処分を受けたことを不服として行政訴訟を提訴するが、敗訴する。そして、約3年間法務省入国管理局の収容施設に収容された後、2019年11月、母国ブラジルへ強制送還された。この時の年齢は32歳であった。

本書は、Tの日本での20年を追跡し、2019年10月に出版した『ある外国人の日本での20年—外国人児童生徒から不法滞在者へ』(下野新聞社)を翻訳したものである。

Tは、上記の本が出版されて1カ月も経たないうちに、母国のブラジルへ強制送還された。Tの家族(両親と弟)は日本に在住しており、強制送還されたTは原則日本に戻ることが出来ないために、家族は事実上分断された。帰国後のTとは、2020年3月に一度だけMessengerで連絡が取れた。Messengerで何度か呼びかけたところ、「はい、私です。元気で頑張っていますが、まだ、仕事が見つかりません。皆さんによろしくお伝えください」と短いメッセージが届いた。帰国後のTと何度か電話で話したという母からの情報によると、物売りなどして何とか暮らしているがホームレス状態にあると思われる。

2020年1月にTから年賀状が届いた。「田巻松雄様へ。新年あけましておめでとうございます。2020年はご家族と一緒に良い年になりますように心よりお祈り申し上げます。私は今頃ブラジルでなれて元気でやっています。どうかご心配なさらないでほしい。Tより」と書かれていた。この年賀状は、Tが、強制送還される前に、新年に届くように準備していたものだ。「私は今頃ブラジルでなれて元気でやっています。どうかご心配なさらないでほしい」との文面にTの優しさが溢れているように感じる。

『ある外国人の日本での20年』は、強制送還される前に、Tに渡すことが出来た。その時には、Tが間もなく強制送還されることは全く予想していなかった。本を出版したことは1つの節目に過ぎず、今後も微力ながら応援したいという気持ちであった。

遠いブラジルに行ってしまい、どこにいるかもわからず連絡も直接取れない今も、Tを応援したい気持ちに変わりはない。応援というよりも、何よりも生き延びてほしい。そして、いつかブラジルで会い、収容所面会室でのアクリル板を挟んだ面会ではなく、直接顔をみながら様々なことを話したいと願っている。

Tは楽しそうに小学校生活を送っていたという。そんなTが中学校で不登校になり、非行・犯罪に走ったのはなぜか。Tの更生を阻んだものは何か。非行・犯罪の事実はTの人生をどこまで縛って良いものなのか。本書は、Tという1人の人物に焦点を当てて、かれの日本での20年を掘り起こす試みである。

翻訳するにあたり、原文を一部加筆・修正した。巻末の参考資料は一部省略した。

本書がTに届くことを願っている。

Contents

Introduction

First Encounter with T

I first encountered T, who was detained at the Higashi-Nihon Immigration Center in Ushiku City, Ibaraki Prefecture, through a letter. The Center, one of two immigrant detention centers in Japan, is a facility for the detention and deportation of illegal residents. The single sheet of T's letter bore a message along these lines: *I have been detained for illegal overstay and will eventually be deported, I've never been to school and have no academic background, isn't there anyone who will help me?* When I saw this letter, at first I thought it must be from a teenager. Words like *illegal overstay, high school dropout, bullying, and protection* stood out. How had he discovered me? What did he want to tell me? Bearing in mind that his Japanese skills seemed rudimentary, I sent a response with character readings added.

The second letter stated that *I've already been in the Higashi-Nihon Immigration Center for eighteen months. I quit school in Japan because I was being bullied. I'd like to go to high school and study but I don't know what to do.* Upon receiving this second letter, I decided to try visiting him. I felt that something drew us together. Just a little while before receiving his first letter, I had shown an American movie called *The Visitor* to my students in a class on international migration. In the movie, an elderly college professor, living alone and closing his heart to others, repeating the same classes every year, and pretending to be "busy" when he is not, encounters a young Syrian and his girlfriend. The young Syrian man is a djembe drummer (djembe being a musical tradition going back to Africa), and as he teaches the fascinated professor to play the drums, they become close.

However, the Syrian is wrongfully arrested for turnstile-jumping when they take the subway. When questioned by the police, his illegal resident status becomes clear and he is sent to an immigration facility. The professor, feeling responsible, tries to help him, while the Syrian's mother (who has come to look for her son when unable to reach him) and his girlfriend pray that this young man with his straightforward desire to spend his life enjoying djembe music will be safe. His mother says that she felt her own failure, when their refugee status application was denied, had condemned her son to illegal residency, but at the time it had made little difference to their lives. They had lived stably for many years with no problems. But then 9/11 happened, and suddenly there was a crackdown on illegal residents…

I was a little uneasy about writing back to T and going to visit him. Careless handling of a letter from someone unknown could lead to serious trouble. However, given my longstanding interest in the lives of foreigners in Japan, I could hardly ignore a direct message. I decided to meet him first and work out how to deal with him then.

The answers to various questions, including the language

issue, came in the third letter: that he would like us to meet once, that he was able to converse in Japanese. My first visit was in June 2018.

It was the first time I had visited Higashi-Nihon Immigration Center. The visitation room where the staff led me kept the visitors and the detainees divided with acrylic panels. The allotted visit time was thirty minutes. I couldn't imagine what kind of a half hour it would be. T didn't seem to be there. I wondered what he was like, recalling the letter in which he had written that he had committed crimes. I was very much on edge.

T was thirty years old. Twenty years had passed since, at age 10, he had come to Japan with his Japanese-Brazilian parents. People of Japanese descent were supposed to be entitled to the status of long-term or permanent residency; when I asked how he had become an illegal immigrant, he said that he had lost his status of residence while in prison. He had stopped attending junior high school after a few months, ending up in juvenile detention, where he had received his junior high school diploma. His parents and younger brother were living in Japan. He said he had found my name and contact information in the endnotes of a book given to the Higashi-Nihon Immigration Center by the Brazilian Consulate General in Tokyo and decided to get in touch with me. The book he mentioned was the *Junior High School Subject Vocabulary Book: Japanese-Portuguese,* produced by the HANDS Project (a support project for foreign children's education). It felt like a strange twist of fate that he had found me through the HANDS Project's vocabulary text.

T's expression was gentle, and his eyes seemed kind. His slow speech in Japanese evoked his longing to try again, to learn again. I could hardly learn anything in a thirty-minute visit, but it was enough to plant the seeds of interest in T's twenty years. One reason was that I felt T's debasement was in some ways typical of foreign children. Books and articles have reported that truancy, delinquency, and criminality are common among foreign children. One notable case is that in which a teacher's casual comment caused a foreign child to stop attending school. To the child—who spoke little Japanese and could not follow the lessons, had no close friends, and was struggling to adjust to school life—the teacher said something along the lines of "Education isn't compulsory for the children of foreigners, so you don't have to come to school if it's too hard." The child took this seriously, stopped attending school, and later fell into delinquency and criminality. It takes so little to keep children out of school, and truancy can be a major trigger for anti-social behavior.

My research interest was piqued at the idea that, by carefully laying out and examining the case of T and his experience of this debasement, I would be able to create a detailed image of the educational problems of foreign children and the backgrounds and contexts of people who had ended up becoming illegal overstayers. I felt that the research required to answer the many questions posed by T's case would be important. I also wanted to task myself with the issue of how to respond to an encounter with someone in a situation like T's.

Hasn't He Been Through Enough Already?

A year passed from my first meeting with T at the Higashi-Nihon Immigration Center in Ushiku City, Ibaraki. I went to visit him a dozen times or more, and we exchanged letters as often. The package which arrived yesterday (June 4, 2019) contained about forty handwritten pages on 400-character paper. I met his mother three times and his father once. I read the trial records from the Tokyo District Court and Tokyo High Court several times. I met several times with the lawyers who had represented him at the trial. During this year, I came to feel, in a few words—Hasn't he been through enough already? He had already been detained at the Immigration Center for two years or so. Why shouldn't he be provisionally released so that he could live with his family?

The facts of his arrest for the malicious crime of convenience store robbery, and his seven years in prison, will not go away; likewise his repeated delinquency (stealing motorcycles, hanging out with a bad crowd, and so on) after dropping out of junior high school, and his two periods of juvenile detention. But how long should these facts remain as constraints on T's life? And what drove T to truancy, delinquency, and crime in the first place?

T was released on parole with ten months of his sentence

to go. Parole is granted to model prisoners who have showed signs of reform toward rehabilitation. “When they granted me parole, I thought my father and mother would come to meet me, but an Immigration Bureau staff member came instead and took me straight to the detention center.” T had applied during his sentence for the renewal of his status as a long-term resident, but the application was denied, making him an illegal overstayer for the remaining four years and ten months of his sentence. If he had been a Japanese citizen, he would have had the opportunity for rehabilitation upon paying his debt to society. However, having become an illegal overstayer while in prison, T was denied that opportunity. Besides this, he was totally unaware that he would be placed in detention. How must he have felt, coming out on parole only to be taken straight to the Immigration Center?

The Immigration Center is a detention facility for deporting illegal residents to their own or a third country; because its purpose is deportation, it has no programs for rehabilitation. While its inmates are permitted a certain amount of freedom of movement for exercise and are able to leave their rooms, they must still remain in their rooms for long periods of time. T’s repeated requests for provisional release, made out of his longing to be a filial son and take care of his brother, were all denied. In this environment, T clung to his study of the law and Japanese as a single ray of hope amid his fear that he would never be released.

The factors defining T’s life so far include his household and school environments, his place within society, interpersonal relations, correction facilities, and the state of immigration law. Meeting T has brought a number of feelings and ideas to light.

This book focuses on the figure of T, a single foreigner, in an attempt to query the significance and issues of the factors which have defined his life. T has granted permission, orally and in writing, for the use of his personal information for research purposes. Descriptions of T are based mainly on records of meetings with him, letters, and trial materials, while those of his mother are based on records of two meetings at her home and on trial materials.

Chapter 1

T's Twenty Years in Japan

A Rough Overview

T was born in Brazil, the child of Brazilian parents of Japanese descent, on January 10, 1988. The general word used for people from Japan who have moved permanently to other countries and for their descendants is Nikkeijin; in T’s case, his grandparents hailed from Japan. His father decided to go as a laborer to Japan when his work in Brazil went poorly; he first arrived there, traveling without his family, in September 1991, and worked in a motorcycle plant for three years before returning to Brazil.

T’s father ran a smoke shop upon his return to Brazil, deciding to go back to Japan when this didn’t work out. He and his wife and T arrived in Japan in February 1998, when T was ten years old. T entered the fourth grade in a Japanese elementary school. As of July 2019, T is 31 years old and detained at the Higashi-Nihon Immigration Center in Ushiku City, Ibaraki. His father (57), mother (52), and brother (12, born in Japan) live in Japan. A rough overview of T’s twenty years in Japan is as follows.

Feb 1, 1998: He arrives at Nagoya Airport and is granted a year’s residency as a long-term resident from a Nagoya Immigration Control Bureau Nagoya Airport Branch immigration officer.

April 1998:He starts fourth grade; age 10.

Nov 1999: His residency status is renewed for three years;

age 11.

April 2001: He starts junior high school and then stops attending school around September of the same year; age 13.

Feb 2002: His residency status is renewed for three years; age 14.

Oct 2003 or so: He enters juvenile detention for multiple counts of delinquency, including extortion and theft; age 15.

Nov 2004 or so: He is paroled from juvenile detention; age 16.

Feb 2005: His residency status is renewed for three years; age 17.

Mar 2005: He enters juvenile detention for delinquency including arson of a residential building,damage to property, theft, and misappropriation of lost property; age 17.

Dec 2006: He is paroled from juvenile detention; age 18.

Dec 2007: His residency status is renewed for one year; age 19.

Mar 2009: His residency status is renewed for three years; age 21.

Jul 2009: He applies for permanent residency; Jan 22, 2010, his application is denied; age 21.

May 2010: He is arrested on suspicion of robbery; Dec 2010, he is found guilty and sentenced to prison for robbery, breaking and entering, theft, and attempted robbery; age 22.

Jan 2012: His father applies on his behalf for renewal of residency status, which is denied; age24.

Feb 2012: He overstays his residence, without being granted renewal or change of status, and becomes an illegal overstayer; age 24.

Aug 2016: Tokyo Immigration Control Bureau officer audits T's violation status at the prison; T requests an oral inquiry by a Special Inquiry Officer; age 28.

Aug 2016: Special Inquiry Officer conducts oral inquiry with T at the prison; T lodges an objection with Minister of Justice; age 28.

Sept 2016: Kanto Regional Parole Board grants parole for October 2016; age 28.

Sept 2016: T is notified that the Tokyo Immigration Control Bureau Director, on the authority of the Minister of Justice, rejects his objection as baseless; age 28.

Oct 2016: Senior Inspector issues a deportation order for T; age 28.

Oct 2016: Immigration Security Officer serves T with deportation order and detains him at Tokyo Immigration Detention Center; age 28.

Mar 2017: Immigration Security Officer detains T at Higashi-Nihon Immigration Center Detention Area; age 29.

Apr 2017: T requests cancellation of the deportation order;

age 29.

Jan 25, 2018: Verdict is issued (Tokyo District Court), T loses; age 30.

2018: T appeals for cancellation of the deportation order; age 30.

Jun 28, 2018: Verdict is issued (Tokyo High Court), T loses.

As of Jun 2019: Detained at Higashi-Nihon Immigration Center.

Truancy and Delinquency

In elementary school, T met another Japanese-Brazilian child who spoke both Japanese and Portuguese, and was able to help him study and teach him some Japanese. There was also a weekly Japanese class specially for Brazilian children. In about a year, T was able to master conversational Japanese. He changed schools twice during elementary school because of his parents' work; the second time was in the second semester of sixth grade.

T started at a Japanese junior high school in April 2001, but stopped attending after just a few months. "I stopped going to junior high around the beginning of September 2001, and went on to drop out. The reason I stopped going to junior high school was that I couldn't follow the lessons and I liked hanging out with a bad crowd who did nothing but bad things" (Inquiry Record, Aug 10, 2016, pp.9-11).

After he stopped attending school, T and his bad crowd committed repeated acts of delinquency. He was arrested and put on probation in family court four times for motorcycle theft and other similar crimes. At fourteen, he was arrested for motorcycle theft and sent to juvenile detention (around November 2003). T spent a year there, receiving his junior high school diploma in the detention center in March 2004. The Ministry of Education instructs schools nationwide to give all students diplomas, on the principle that students undergoing compulsory education must not be held back or expelled. Therefore, what are referred to as "graduates in name only" exist in Japan, having graduated from junior high school without actually attending it, due to truancy or illness.

After his parole from juvenile detention (November 2004), T returned to his family's home and found a job at a local bakery, which he quit after a week. Six months after his release, in March 2005, he was once again put into juvenile detention for arson of a residential building, damage to property, theft, and misappropriation of lost property. "Arson of a residential building" referred to setting fire to a police box. T was once again paroled on December 18, 2006. He returned to his family and worked as a hotel cleaner, at an automobile parts factory, as a construction worker, at a bar and so on.

Crime and Punishment

From October 2009 or so through May 2010, T committed robbery and theft multiple times with three Brazilians as well as Japanese. He had gotten to know C, the Brazilian who took the lead in the robberies, around April 2008 when working at the automobile parts plant; they became friends through their shared experience in juvenile detention, and C introduced him to the other two Brazilians. T was arrested on May 27, 2010, for one count of attempted robbery, three robberies, and six counts of theft, and imprisoned on December 16. The prosecution called for a sentence of nine years; based on his youth and lack of a previous record, the judge reduced the sentence to seven.

From Long-Term Resident to Illegal Overstayer

T's family applied for permanent residency on July 27, 2009; their application was denied on January 22, 2010. At this point, T's status of residence as a long-term resident lasted until February 1, 2012. In January 2012, while T was in prison, his father applied on his behalf for renewal of his residence status, but it was denied; as a result, he became an illegal overstayer and thus subject to deportation on February 1, 2012, while still in prison. T remained in prison with the status of an illegal overstayer for some four and a half years.

Out on Parole

On August 12, 2016, the Kanto Regional Parole Board granted T parole with 10 months of his sentence to go (his parole date was October 27). Parole is a release granted as an opportunity for rehabilitation to prisoners in correctional facilities before the end of their sentence, in order for them to return smoothly to life in society; it may be granted to prisoners serving criminal sentences as well as to youths in juvenile detention. Parole is usually considered about 80% into the sentence. In T's case, his parole was granted when he had served almost 90% of his sentence.

In response to the deportation order issued on October 25, 2016, T was detained at the Tokyo Immigration Control Bureau on October 27, the day of his parole. On March 10, 2017, he was transferred to the Higashi-Nihon Immigration Center.

Trial

On April 24, 2017, T sued the governmental representatives (Director and Senior Inspector of the Tokyo Immigration Control Bureau) in administrative court, requesting the cancellation of his deportation order. T was demanding the cancellation of the decision not to grant special residence status to him as plaintiff and of the deportation order based thereon, on the grounds that it exceeded or constituted an illegal abuse of discretionary authority. The trial took place at the Tokyo District and High Courts, both ending in defeat for the plaintiff (the High Court judgment was passed on June 28, 2018). T did not appeal to the Supreme Court, and thus the trial came to an end.

Detention

Foreigners are detained based on either detention or deportation orders. While a detention order enables its subject to be held for up to 60 days, a deportation order has no upper limit and enables long-term detention. At this time there are two detention centers intended for long-term detention (the Higashi-Nihon Immigration Center in Ushiku and the Omura Immigration Center in Omura City, Nagasaki). T was transferred to the Higashi-Nihon Immigration Center on March 10, 2017, so that as of June 2019 he had already been there for over two years.

There is a temporary release system applicable to detainees in the center. Temporary release indicates allowing detainees their freedom for a given period of time, as an exception under certain conditions, such as illness or other unavoidable situations. T's repeated applications for temporary release were all turned down. As of June 2019, he was in the process of applying a seventh time for temporary release.

T's Hopes

T very much regrets having strayed from the path; his greatest hope is to remain in Japan. "I am sorry that I committed a criminal act and broke the law. However, I want to get out of the Higashi-Nihon Immigration Center as soon as I can, but Immigration Control won't let me out. I don't know when I can get out, but I believe I will be let out someday" (T's third letter). T's conversation and his letters often touch on his family and high school. "The hardest thing is that I can't see my family. I always think of my family when I'm unhappy. That way I can tell myself I have to overcome it. When I get out of here, I will work hard as an act of thanks to my family for watching over me for thirty years." T is grateful to his family for refusing to abandon him, no matter what has become of him.

"I want to see my family, who have never turned away from me. I think they've had it hardest of all. I want to be a good son. My mother is a kind person. I talk to her on the phone every Sunday. My father is strict. But when I bowed to him and apologized, he forgave me. He told me to come home when I got out of the Immigration Center. I haven't seen my parents in about a year and four months. When I was in Tokyo, they came to see me. They tried to come to Ushiku too, but they got lost and couldn't make it and felt really bad. My mother is sick right now and the doctor told her to stay at home and rest. So it's hard for them to come either by car or by public transport like trains. My father is supporting the family. My brother's in his first year of junior high school. I haven't seen him in about a year and eight months. I don't want him to make the same mistakes I did, so if I can get out on temporary release, I want to talk to him so he understands."

T said that if granted temporary release, he wants to attend high school or college, his dream from an early age. His letters touch on this longing as well. "Right now, I've learned that life is studying all your life" (second letter). "I want to get out of here as soon as possible and keep on studying" (fourth letter). "High school and staying in Japan are my only hope" (fifth letter). He says "Other countries don't keep people in detention so long the way Japan does. Personally, two of my roommates got temporary release. I can see hope for myself and the people around me. I want more people to know about this situation. I think most Japanese people don't know that so many foreigners are detained. So I want them to know."

T's Future

In response to his defeat as the plaintiff in the trial calling for the cancellation of his deportation order, T was left with only two ways out of the Higashi-Nihon Immigration Center. One was temporary release, but given that all his applications to date had been refused, he had little hope that continued applications would bear fruit in the future. The other was to leave Japan. If he decided to leave and applied for temporary release in order to see his family first, his application might be approved. However, if he returned to Brazil, he would face another cruel aspect of reality: "Persons who have committed a crime and been imprisoned for one year or more (excluding political crimes) are refused entry to Japan for an unlimited period." That is, T would be essentially unable to return to Japan. Based on T's family's nearly twenty years in Japan and his mother's current poor health, his return to Brazil would mean tearing the family in two. More to the point, would T himself be able to make a life in Brazil, where he had not lived for twenty years and which was hardly his home country any more in terms of language, culture, and human connections?

Summary

Theft, arson, robbery, two periods of juvenile detention, prison, illegal overstay. Ugly words overshadow T's twenty years. Theft is the crime of stealing others' property, punishable by up to ten years' imprisonment. Robbery is the crime of stealing others' property through assault or intimidation, or illegally obtaining profit or enabling a third party to do so thus, punishable by five years' imprisonment or more. Arson is sometimes punished as severely as murder, as it may lead to multiple deaths, injuries, or damage to property. Setting fire to a building in which people are present is considered arson of inhabited buildings.

T came to Japan when he was ten years old, entering fourth grade. His mother says that he seemed to enjoy attending elementary school. What drove him to delinquency and crime? What were juvenile detention centers and prison like for him? What kept him from rehabilitation? What lay behind his long-term detention? Let us consider T's twenty years in greater detail, keeping these questions in mind.

Chapter 2

Truancy, Delinquency, and Juvenile Detention

Coming to Japan

T was brought to Japan by his parents in 1998, at the age of ten, when he entered fourth grade. He knew no Japanese at all. He describes his feelings at the time thus: "I didn't have any option but to come, but after a while I started to like Japan." The safety and security of daily life appealed to him. His mother also says that going to Japan had been a dream of hers which she was happy to realize. They had originally planned to return to Brazil after a few years, she recounts, but decided to stay because T seemed to be enjoying life in Japan.

"When we first came to Japan, T couldn't speak Japanese at all. He knew some Portuguese, but he wasn't a very talkative child to begin with. Maybe because he had a little bit of a stammer, he used to stumble on his words sometimes. So I think it might have been hard for him to talk. But in elementary school, he was happy and energetic about going to school. There were other Brazilian and Peruvian children in the elementary school where he began. I think he got to like Japan a little at a time through going to school" (T's mother).

At his elementary school, T encountered W, another third-generation Japanese-Brazilian. Fluent in both Japanese and Portuguese, W was able to help him study and learn Japanese. There was also a special Japanese class once a week specifically for Brazilian children. According to T, he mastered everyday conversation in Japanese within a year, making Japanese friends as well. Sometimes he was left out or quarreled with his friends, but while in elementary school he faced no serious problems. However, changing schools twice made it difficult for him to make friends. The second time was in the second semester of sixth grade. T recounts that "coming to Japan where the culture and language were both completely different, and having to change elementary schools three times [author's note: counting his first school as the first change], I had trouble fitting in and ended up going to junior high school without making any friends" (Statement, November 11, 2010, p.1).

There seem to have been no notable family troubles either. "Our son would come home first, and he would be there when we got home. We ate dinner together. But sometimes we had to be out late. We were doing shift work and had to do overtime then as well, so sometimes we would get home late. In elementary school, he really liked studying and always went to school. He never ever gave us any trouble" (T's mother).

From Truancy to Delinquency

While T entered a Japanese junior high school, he stopped attending within a matter of months. In junior high school, there were no special Japanese-language classes. T feels that he stopped attending because he couldn't follow the lessons, he couldn't make friends, and he was miserable due to being bullied. It also made a difference that he had no close friends to start junior high with. "I went on to junior high school, but I couldn't understand the lessons and I didn't have any friends at school, so I stopped attending in the second semester of my first year. I didn't have any friends at the Japanese school and I was so lonely" (Statement Record, February 3, 2015, p.7).

"I was bullied at junior high school, not just by Japanese but by other Brazilians. I couldn't ask my homeroom teacher for help. I wanted to tell my parents, but I didn't. That was when I got into a bad crowd and started hanging out at video game arcades and places like that. My bad friends didn't fight or bully one another." Unable to enjoy school, T must simultaneously have drifted away from school and fallen in with a bad crowd. "The bullying began in junior high school. Everything changed when he started junior high. We really didn't know that there were children at that school who stole things, stole motorbikes, or got violent, we didn't know he had friends like that until he stopped attending school. His bad friends were a group of Japanese delinquents. He didn't know how dangerous it would be to get involved with them, he probably just thought 'I live in Japan, so I have to do what they tell me.' My husband and I were working all the time at that point, so we gradually stopped noticing the changes in our son. So we didn't understand anything that was going on until he said he wanted to quit school" (T's mother). "Our son was afraid to have us find out what his friends were like. He knew his father would be angry to find he was involved with a group of delinquents. So he never told us that he was spending time with these friends" (T's mother).

"I went into the school two or three times. His teacher was very worried, asking us what was happening. But I think the teacher must have known at some level why our son wasn't coming to school anymore. Because the delinquent boys were in the same class, in other classes [at the same school]. And there were others outside school who were their friends and involved with children at the school that way. The teacher must have known too. But nobody at the school told us anything at all. I learned about it from a Peruvian who had a child at the same school, because her son was part of the group too."

Before he stopped attending school, T had several conversations with his homeroom teacher and his parents (he served as interpreter). At first, both were against his leaving school, but his parents gradually came to feel that he didn't need to force himself to go. His homeroom teacher was firmly opposed, saying that it would cause T himself trouble in the future if he stopped attending school.

T describes the situation at the time thus. "I stopped going to junior high because I couldn't follow the lessons and I was having fun hanging out with a bad crowd who did bad things. This is what I did after I stopped going to junior high. My bad friends and I rode around on stolen motorbikes and had fun. When I was thirteen, I was arrested by the police along with my bad friends for stealing bike parts and shrine offerings, and put on probation in court. Then again, when I was fourteen, I was arrested twice by the police for stealing motorbikes with my bad friends and put on probation twice in family court. And then I was arrested again when I was fifteen for extortion and sniffing paint thinner along with my bad friends, and put on probation in family court. And when I was fifteen I was arrested by the police for stealing a motorbike and sent to juvenile detention. I kept on committing crimes even though I was on probation because I didn't want the bad friends I hung out with to hate me because I wouldn't go along with them, and because I needed money to have fun with. My parents yelled at me every time I was arrested, but I was in the rebellious stage and I couldn't take in what they were telling me" (Inquiry Record, Aug 10, 2016, pp.9-10).

T's personality began to change as he fell in with the delinquent group. "He changed completely when he started junior high school. He started hanging out with that delinquent group, and he became rebellious, like a different person. He didn't throw things, but his temper was shorter. I wanted to know what was wrong, but he wouldn't tell me" (T's mother). In October 2003, at the age of 15, T was sent to juvenile detention for delinquency including multiple counts of intimidation and theft.

The Juvenile Detention Center

Juvenile detention centers are facilities which conduct corrective education under the jurisdiction of the Ministry of Justice, detaining mainly young people who have been sentenced to juvenile detention as a protective measure in family court. As of April 1, 2018, there were 51 juvenile detention centers (including six sub-centers) in Japan (*White Paper on Crime, 2018*). The purpose of juvenile detention centers is to provide opportunities for rehabilitation, behavioral improvement, and smooth reintegration through measures contributing to the healthy development of the detainees such as appropriate corrective education suited to their characteristics. Corrective education is at the core of the measures taken in juvenile detention, with instruction provided to detainees in the five areas of lifestyle guidance, vocational guidance, school subject instruction, physical education, and special activities. As an overview of the process from initial detention to release, there is a graduated system in which the achievement of educational goals at each level is evaluated, based upon which the detainee may or may not advance to the next level. The system is composed of three levels: Level 3 (guidance toward developing the will to resolve one's own issues), Level 2 (specific guidance toward resolving issues), and Level 1 (guidance for a smooth transfer back to life in society). Detainees who have reached Level 1 are eligible for release.

In T's case, having repeatedly committed acts of delinquency while on probation, he was sent to juvenile detention. His juvenile detention center had introduced a "subject curriculum for detainees who have not completed compulsory education" in June 1977; as of June 2015, when the new Juvenile Training School Act came into force, the center officially offered compulsory education curricula I and II as well as social adaptation curricula I and II. While it has not been possible to confirm with the treatment records from T's admission, it is thought that he was treated as a "foreigner or other person requiring consideration in treatment different from the Japanese" because of his poor Japanese skills. Long-term measures were taken, with the educational period (detention period) being about a year on average. T's prefecture had no juvenile detention centers, so he was assigned to a center about four hours by train from his home. Based on the center's pamphlet, here is an overview of the contents of correctional education and a day in the life of a detainee.

A typical day proceeds as follows. 7:00: Get up/wash face/attend to physical needs/clean room; 7:40: breakfast/recess; 8:20: morning homeroom; 9:10: morning assembly/morning classes (subject instruction, vocational guidance, education for new detainees, etc.); 12:00: lunch/recess; 13:10: afternoon assembly/afternoon classes (specified lifestyle guidance, club activities, physical education/exercise, etc.); 17:00: dinner/recess; 18:00: attend to physical needs/reflection/diary writing; 19:00: independent activities, etc.; 20:00: leisure (television, studying, etc.); 21:00: go to bed.

Subject instruction includes basics-oriented instruction, supplementary instruction for those planning to take high school entrance exams, and instruction aimed at the High School Equivalency Exam. Vocational guidance is offered to high school dropouts and also includes instruction aimed at obtaining vocational qualifications. As of 2018, 31 detainees held Hazardous Material Engineer's qualifications, 16 had passed the Abacus Proficiency Exam, 43 the Japan Kanji

Aptitude Test, and 13 the CS Skills Test (word processing level 3). Yearly events include graduation, cherry blossom viewing, a soccer tournament, the first pool swim of the year, a swimming tournament, Sports Day, a softball exchange game, festivals, and so on.

T remembers his time in juvenile detention thus. "After we ate breakfast, school started at nine o'clock. We had Japanese [for native speakers] for an hour or so, honestly it was hard. I guess I would have to say I didn't understand the class. There were no special classes and I didn't understand anything. But I tried for a year. School was over at eleven and then we'd go back to the dorm and have lunch at twelve. ... Before dinner we had diary-writing time, but I didn't know enough Japanese and at first I was writing just one line at a time. One of the teachers lent me a Japanese dictionary for elementary schools, so I learned a lot of Japanese that way. From six to seven, we had study time. At first it was hard because I couldn't understand the Japanese. I spent so much time asking the teachers questions. I must have asked them a million times about words in Japanese. From seven o'clock we had free time, but there was a strict rule that we weren't supposed to talk to each other. ... I remember calling out "Let's go get 'em!" at the last Sports Day before I left. That made a big impression on me. I wasn't the leader but I was always the best at sports, so the teacher always chose me. I carried the flag and we won by a lot of points" (letter, partially corrected).

Based on the text above as well talking to him in person,

it seems that T found life in the juvenile detention center strict but essentially enjoyable. His phrase "because I couldn't understand Japanese" and his struggle to write more than a single line at a time in his diary at first suggest that his Japanese reading and writing skills were still very poor, but "asking the teachers a million times about words in Japanese" conveys his desire to learn. Besides this, the T who shouted "Let's go get 'em!" to his teammates seems to have found, in a sense, a place where he felt at home in communal life.

Life After Parole from Juvenile Detention

T left juvenile detention on parole around November 2004 and returned to his parents' house. Parole in this case indicates the measures taken when the detainee has reached the highest level of treatment within the detention center and has been evaluated as suitable for release, or when it is thought that release is especially required for improvement and rehabilitation. Parole is granted on the authority of the Regional Parole Board, which makes a decision with consideration to the results of the probation office's arrangements regarding factors such as the detainee's grades and evaluation at the center, their home environment, their guardians' attitudes, and so on, as well as an interview with the detainee him/herself by an inspection committee member. Most detainees are permanently released through parole. In 2017 the number of releasees was 2,475, of whom 2,469 (99.8%) had been paroled (*White Paper on Crime, 2018*).

Youths on parole are consigned to probation, a measure intended to support their rehabilitation in society. Their daily lives are taken account of through interviews with probation officers, national civil servants with specialized expertise, as well as volunteer probation officers. Youth probation periods are, in principle, two years or until they turn twenty.

T's mother remembers clearly that a probation officer visited their house several times, encouraging and advising him not to spend time with the bad friends of his past and to stay home and study as much as possible. About three months after leaving juvenile detention on parole, T began to look for work through the HelloWork labor bureau. He had always liked making things and once hoped to open a bakery of his own, so he found a job at a bakery. However, he quit the job within a week.

T's mother speaks of this period as below. "He was working at a bread factory. He quit in just a week partly because of the early hours, but mostly because of his bad friends. They wouldn't leave my son alone. They knew he was working at the bread factory, and even so they'd come into my house and look for my son to go and hang around with them. They came all the time, every day, morning and night, to bang on the door and yell "Where's T at?!". It was a nightmare. They even came in the second-floor window. And my son was working! How could he stay calm during work when they were doing this? He's never had trouble working. He was doing the job. But he quit the bakery because he was out with those bad friends until three AM, so he couldn't get up in the morning. I think he quit so he could stay out at night with them. He couldn't tell his bad friends no. He knew it was wrong and he still couldn't say no to them" (T's mother).

After leaving the bread factory, T was unable to find another job and began to spend all his time with his bad friends. It took time before his parents realized this. "At the time, we were working overtime a lot, and we had no chance to notice. He was coming home late, so we thought he must be out with friends, but we had no idea it was the same bad crowd, doing the same bad things again" (T's mother).

Second Juvenile Detention and Life After Parole

On March 1, 2005, T was sentenced to juvenile detention in family court for acts of delinquency including arson of inhabited buildings, damage to property, theft, and misappropriation of lost property. Around March 4, he entered juvenile detention once again, just a few months after being paroled. Regarding the charge of arson, he recalls "Two Japanese guys and I spread gasoline around and set fire to it, kind of for fun."

T's second juvenile detention center handled "seriously delinquent youths, such as those with antisocial values and behavior tendencies," "foreigners and others requiring consideration in treatment different from the Japanese," and "criminals under 16." The treatment curriculum for foreign youths had been established in 2003.

Vocational guidance offered included (1) vocational lifestyle planning guidance (basic etiquette as an adult in society, clerical skills, computer use), (2) vocational guidance in support of independence (pottery, woodwork, service skills), and (3) vocational ability development guidance (office automation, study to qualify as a hazardous material engineer, sand rammer operator, crane operator, forklift operator, and Japanese word processor).

A visit in June 2019 found that the international section, composed of detainees with foreign nationality, included three Chinese, one Nepalese, and one Colombian. “The international section, composed of detainees who are foreigners and others requiring consideration in treatment different from the Japanese, offers Japanese-language education and the guidance required to enhance understanding of Japanese culture and customs and cultivate the awareness and attitudes required of a sound adult in society” (pamphlet).

T recalls this detention center thus. “I had a single room. There was one other Brazilian but he was released, so I don’t know what he’s up to now. After two or three months of basic training, I studied pottery in the pottery class. A few months later I went to learn office automation. My Japanese wasn’t very good, so I studied a lot. I still remember using the *Minna no Nihongo* textbook. There was a laptop I could use, so I studied Japanese every day. Studying for a year really helped. I mean, on July 21, 2006, I got my forklift qualifications and another one too. I got qualified as a crane operator. I was really happy. I felt as if I'd achieved something. That's what it feels like to 'achieve a goal'" (letter, partially corrected).

T spent about eighteen months at his second detention center before being paroled in December 2006 and returning to his parents' home. In January 2007, he found a job as a hotel cleaner. There were no days off, and mornings were early. He kept working while hoping to quit so that he could see his family more. After working at the hotel for nine months, he found a job at a factory making automotive parts, with better wages: this company paid him about 200,000 yen a month. During this period, T paid 5,000 yen a month in compensation for the police box and gave his parents 110,000 yen monthly. However, around April 2008, "the factory, which made car parts as a subcontractor, suddenly stopped getting orders because the large manufacturers were struggling. They fired a lot of us foreign workers." (Statement, November 11, 2010, p.2). He had worked there for about seven months.

Summary

Most second-generation immigrants like T, flung into Japanese society as school-age children and understanding virtually nothing from Japanese on up, begin their new lives with serious anxiety. In T's case, he left junior high school shortly after starting, for reasons including trouble with classes, lack of friends, and bullying, and also fell in with a group of delinquent Japanese. He behaved rebelliously toward his parents as well. He may have felt dissatisfied or resentful toward his parents for bringing him to a place where he could not follow his lessons and ended up bullied. With no place he could relax, whether at school or at home, T found himself feeling at home in his bad crowd of Japanese friends. "Without knowing whether he belonged to Japan or to Brazil, unable to speak either Japanese or his mother tongue properly, there was no place T felt at home except with his group of friends who did bad things" (T's mother's Statement, September 1, 2017, p.2).

T remembers working hard during his year in juvenile detention. Having left junior high school after just a few months, he must have found the detention center a valuable opportunity to study Japanese, among other things. Finding the bakery job after his first parole also indicates his desire for rehabilitation. However, unable to refuse invitations from his bad friends, he was drawn back once again into delinquency. His mother remembers the period when the Japanese delinquent group was relentlessly trying to drag T out with them as a nightmare. T must have found it difficult to cut ties with the bad friends, the one place he had felt at home. In response to the idea of being disliked by his bad friends, T often recounts his unease about losing the only friends he had and his fear of what they might do to him.

T's life after his second parole from juvenile detention, working as a hotel cleaner and in a factory, was stable for over a year. He attended work reliably and engaged in no antisocial behavior. Based on these facts, no argument can be made that

T was unwilling or unable to work. His bad luck came in the form of the sudden downsizing of foreign workers at the plant where the conditions had been good. From then on, he was unable to find long-term work.

Visiting three juvenile detention centers, including those where T had been detained, I had a strong sense of the solid protection and painstaking education taking place there. However, some youths are unable to make use in society of the corrective education they underwent in all seriousness, falling into recidivism. According to the *White Paper on Crime 2018*, the rate of repeat detention (the rate of juvenile detention releasees sentenced once again to detention within a given period) in 2013 was 10.5% within two years and 15.1% within five years.

Chapter 3

Guilty Verdict and Illegal Overstay

Robbery

After losing his factory job in April 2008, T changed jobs often. It must have been extremely difficult for him to find work as a young foreigner with education only up to the level of junior high school whose Japanese was minimal. “From around May 2008 to April 2009, he couldn’t find a steady job but sometimes he’d come home in dirty work clothes, so I think he had some kind of part-time job of his own then” (T’s mother’s, Inquiry Record, June 1, 2010, p.9).

The Lehman crash occurred in September 2008, resulting in a heavy blow to Japan’s economy. Thereafter, due to the large-scale firing of South Americans of Japanese descent, the numbers of Nikkeijin (foreigners with Japanese heritage) applicants at HelloWork offices shot up, reaching 20 times those of the previous year at their peak.

A few months after T lost his job, in a concatenation of bad luck, his father was fired from the company where he had worked for many years. T’s father went out all but daily looking for work, but—given the recession, his illiteracy in Japanese, and his age—was unable to find a job for some time. From this point on, T’s parents were no longer able to provide him with the previously monthly allowance of 2,000 to 3,000 yen. Both T and his parents were in economic trouble.

In May 2009, for all intents and purposes T ran away from home, unable to find a stable job and tired of being scolded by his parents. A yakuza group picked him up while he wandered aimlessly, and for some months he received an occasional allowance in return for cleaning and cooking. He made too little even to afford a prepaid cell phone card. It was in October 2009 that T received a phone call from C. T had met C, another Brazilian, at his previous factory job. "I met C at the plant. Because we had experience of the same background, going through juvenile detention, he made me feel kind of familiar and happy, and we got along."

"On October 5, 2009, defendants C and M and N, having watched an online news video at C's house in which a man armed with a knife threatened a store clerk and stole one million yen, discussed robbing a convenience store for money to live on. Believing that having more people would make it easier to threaten the clerk and receive money, C suggested to M and N that they include T, and upon their agreement called him to invite him along" (Opening Statement, October 14, 2010, p.2).

"C called me and said 'Want to come over and hang out?' so I did. We watched some convenience store robbery videos on YouTube, mostly just fooling around. We got the idea from there that if we committed robbery ourselves, it would be easy and we could get a fortune. None of the four of us who did it had any money; we were living from day to day. When people who are struggling on account of not having money talk together, it's easy to believe because you want the money so bad that if you just rob someone it will all work out. We didn't make any careful plans or anything" (Statement, November 11, 2010, p.3).

C and the others decided what store to rob. Early on October 6, 2009, the day after watching the videos, T and the two others attempted robbery. It was an impulsive crime, based on the casual belief that they could pull it off themselves. This time, the store clerk called the police and their plan failed. However, undeterred, they attempted three more robberies between then and the following May (January, March, and May 2010).

In March 2009, T had met a Filipino woman through a friend's introduction. From then on, he seems to have felt more strongly about settling down to live right. While he participated in the fourth robbery, he refused C's invitation to a fifth. Deciding to look for work in Tokyo if there was none in the area, he left home. His initial Tokyo-based plans changed when he learned that the Filipino woman had moved to the North Kanto area, where he went to stay with her and found a job as a construction worker. On May 25, he told his mother on the phone that he had good news: he was working at a construction site near Tokyo and living with someone. Two days later, while eating out with the woman, he was arrested.

"I should have listened to my parents. I couldn't turn down bad invitations from my bad friends. I wish I'd been tougher and told them no. I was afraid of what they might not do to me if I turned them down, and I didn't want to lose my friends" (Oral Inquiry Record, August 31, 2016, pp.7-8).

Guilty Verdict

In May 2010, T was arrested on suspicion of one count of attempted robbery, three of robbery, and six of theft. For the four counts of robbery (one attempted), he was complicit with another Brazilian. The prosecutor called for a sentence of nine years in prison, on the grounds that "there is nothing that can excuse his thoughtless and careless behavior, having decided on robbery and stealing from cars when in money trouble while still young and fully able to earn a living by honest work."

The defense argued for a lenient sentence, given that he had not received sufficient education, that unemployment had cut off his earnings and essentially led to the incidents in question, that C had been the leader in the four robbery incidents, and that T regretted his actions deeply and was eager for rehabilitation. The District Court, stating that "the crimes were thoughtlessly undertaken out of a need for funds for daily life and leisure, with nothing excusable in their motivation and significant criminal responsibility on the part of the defendant," handed down a verdict thus: "admitting various points in the defendant's favor, such as the failure of the first robbery, the fact that some of the stolen items were returned to the victim(s), the fact that the defendant has confessed to his crimes and shown regret such as sending a written apology to the victim(s), his youth at age 22, his clean previous record, and his mother's oath in court to monitor his behavior in future," T was sentenced to seven years in prison out of the nine demanded (Verdict, December 16, 2010).

Prisons are state-run penal institutions detaining criminals who have broken the law and been found guilty in court and sentenced to imprisonment (with or without penal labor). While juvenile detention centers are established in order to rehabilitate youth and mainly conduct corrective education, prisons are places to atone for crimes and serve sentences—in other words, to be punished. Penalties for criminals found guilty in court include death sentences, custodial sentences, and fines. Of these, custodial sentences refer to the imprisonment (with or without penal labor) or detention of the criminal. The criminal is detained in a prison, detention center, or other penal facility with major limitations placed on their freedom of movement and lifestyle (thus leading to the Japanese term jiyukei or "freedom penalty"). Detention in a penal institution essentially rules out movement on one's own terms until the sentence is over. The sentence of imprisonment with penal labor is intended to increase the inmate's desire to work and enable them to acquire vocationally useful knowledge and skills, requiring them to work eight hours a day, five days a week with no alternative.

Prisons are institutions of punishment, but also possess rehabilitation programs for their inmates, with various initiatives intended to prevent recidivism after release. I have been told that prisons have changed notably in character over the last ten to fifteen years: that is, the rehabilitation and sound return to society of their inmates has become a major objective, reinforcing their role as corrective institutions. T's prison was for men only, detaining those with advanced criminal inclinations and sentences under ten years, foreigners requiring treatment different from the Japanese, and those sentenced to imprisonment without labor. In 2001, they began accepting foreign inmates able to understand Japanese.

While stunned by his sentencing to seven years in prison, T also seems to have seen it as a chance for redemption and rehabilitation. "When I heard the sentence of seven years in prison, everything went black. But this pitch-black seven-year verdict was actually a saving grace, although ordinary people wouldn't understand how. The thing is that my rehabilitated life began with this arrest. God decided that I should be here and that I should spend seven years in prison, I still think this. If I hadn't accepted that seven-year verdict, I wouldn't be the person I am now," he recounts in a letter. "I am still glad I was arrested. In Ezekiel 33:11, God says 'I have no pleasure in the death of the wicked, but that the wicked turn from his way and live. Turn, turn from your evil ways!'" T also recalls that in prison he worked and studied hard. He feels that prison gave him the chance at rehabilitation that, knowing he should reject his bad friends and bad behavior but unable to do so, he had never had before.

Life in Prison and on Parole

The Kanto Regional Parole Board granted T parole on August 12, 2016. "Parole is granted. The date of parole is to be

October 27, 2018. Items to be observed specially while under probation during parole, in the event of parole according to this decision, are: 1. Cutting off contact of any kind whatsoever with accomplices; 2. Cutting off contact of any kind whatsoever with criminal organizations" ("Decision Notification"). "Other reference items" in Appendix (2) called for "returning home accompanied by the guarantor or their representative if at all possible." Parole was granted for the point at which about ten months of T's sentence would remain.

Parole inquiries and decisions are handled not by the corrective institution where the inmate is imprisoned but by Regional Parole Boards and probation offices under the jurisdiction of the Ministry of Justice. The Kanto Regional Parole Board, located in Saitama City, has jurisdiction over eleven prefectures (Tokyo, Kanagawa, Saitama, Chiba, Ibaraki, Tochigi, Gunma, Shizuoka, Yamanashi, Nagano, and Niigata) and handles inquiries into whether or not to grant parole. According to Article 31 of the Regulations on Parole, Temporary and Provisional Release, and Probation, the judgment on whether to grant parole is based on overall consideration of various factors including the inmate's record of behavior within the corrective institution, their mental and physical health, the factors and content of their crime or delinquency, the environment awaiting them outside prison, and their future life plans. Article 31 (Criteria for Granting Parole) states that the inmate must show remorse, must be willing to attempt rehabilitation, must not be a recidivism risk, and must be acceptable as a parolee by society.

Let us consider T's life in prison. The prison's record of internment for T, an inmate sentenced to imprisonment with penal labor, reads as follows. "Punishments: 5 times," "Behavior during sentence: Lack of motivation with regard to work and improvement guidance, such as repeated rule-breaking," "Character: Highly self-assertive and prone to losing his temper." In response to an inquiry about T's punishments (number, date, content, reason), the Tokyo Immigration Control Bureau Director responded on June 16, 2017, with a "Response to Inquiry" listing six punishments as below.

1. June 6, 2011: Seven days' confinement. Idleness (refusal to take part in factory work, with no valid reason)
2. September 8, 2011: Warning. Unauthorized laundry (unauthorized use of water)
3. January 26, 2012: Seven days' confinement. Idleness (refusal to take part in factory work, with no valid reason)
4. April 16, 2012: Ten days' confinement. Unauthorized transfer of goods (unauthorized bestowal of goods)
5. June 9, 2014: Fifteen days' confinement. Fighting (fight with cellmate in cell)
6. August 28, 2014: Seven days' confinement. Unauthorized laundry (laundering clothes without permission, unauthorized use of water)

Disciplinary confinement is one of the penalties for inmates regulated in the Act on Penal Detention Facilities, in which inmates are confined in their cells for up to 30 days (up to 60 days for adults over the age of 20 in serious circumstances), with the use of self-supplied articles, participation in religious services, access to books, visits, and receipt of letters prohibited. Five of T's six penalties involved confinement. Incidentally, T's record of internment as an inmate sentenced to imprisonment with labor and the Director's inquiry response were used by the defense (i.e. the Tokyo Immigration Control Bureau Director and Senior Inspector) in the trial addressed in the following chapter to argue that T's attitude during his sentence had been poor. "During his prison sentence, the plaintiff was punished six times and showed a 'lack of motivation with regard to work and improvement guidance, such as repeated rule-breaking,' indicating a poor attitude to his imprisonment" (Response, July 6, 2017, p.21).

T recalls his punishments thus. "I was punished six times in prison, but three of them weren't because I did anything bad; it was that I wasn't getting along with my cellmates and wanted to change cells, and the officer in charge said I had to go to the punishment block to get my room changed, so that's what I did. Also, I got punished for unauthorized laundry, because I washed towels even though the prison rule was that you couldn't wash towels with soap. There was a fight too, because the other guy hit me, so I had to fight back to defend myself. None of them were serious punishments, and I had fewer than most of the inmates" (Statement, October 4, 2017, p.2).

A former penal officer now working at a juvenile detention center says that people who have come to find the personal relations within the communal life in their cells or their factory work intolerable may sometimes deliberately refuse to work in order to be punished with confinement. They will be transferred to a different group if expected to refuse to work once again when returned to the original one after confinement. T's idleness is thought to have stemmed from this situation.

A former Kanto Regional Parole Board coordination officer discusses parole thus. "For inmates, the discussion begins upon a parole consideration request from the prison director. The coordination officer's job is to conduct interviews, investigate the behavior of the potential parolee in prison, and report on the results. In response, a three-member committee handles the inquiry and decision. Parole with ten months to go out of a seven-year sentence seems to indicate that the inmate's efforts in various prison rehabilitation programs have been recognized. Quite a few inmates serve full sentences without receiving parole. The state report indicates six cautions and a potentially poor attitude, but rule-breaking covers a multitude of sins and cautions can have various causes. Anything from actually refusing to take part in penal labor to giving another prisoner some of your own food, there are any number of levels, from the really appalling through the very mild. Being drawn into a fight by another prisoner, that's not unusual either. But being granted parole to begin with certainly means that the prisoner's efforts have been recognized. There are various legal criteria for parole, which have to have been cleared."

From Parole to the Immigration Control Facility

Parole is generally considered to be the granting of an opportunity for rehabilitation. However, for T this opportunity was not available. Deportation proceedings were put in place against him as an illegal overstayer, and as of October 27, 2016, the day of his parole, he was detained in an immigration control facility in Shinagawa, Tokyo. T's application for renewal of his status as a long-term resident had not been granted, and as of February 1, 2012, he had become an illegal overstayer while still in prison.

Article 24 of the Immigration Control Act regulates foreigners who are subject to deportation. The following two items are relevant to T: "(b) A person who has stayed in Japan beyond the period of stay authorized without obtaining an extension or change thereof" and "(i) ...[A] person who has been sentenced on or after November 1, 1951, to imprisonment with work or imprisonment for life or for a period of not less than 1 year."

Deportation refers to the denial of landing permission to a foreigner for whom sufficient reasons apply, or the forcible expulsion from Japan of a foreigner considered unfavorable for Japan due to disruption of Japanese society upon entry or disruption of the orderly process of immigration control. Deportation proceedings begin upon discovery of violation of the Immigration Control Act. The general process includes a violation investigation (by an immigration security officer), a violation inspection (by an immigration inspector), an oral inquiry (by a special inspector, with objection to the Minister of Justice if dissatisfied with the results of the inquiry), the decision of the Minister of Justice, and the deportation itself. However, the Special Permission to Stay in Japan system is positioned within these proceedings; even when the Minister of Justice rules that the objection made is not valid, they may grant special permission to remain in Japan to the suspect in question. This special ministerial permission is determined based on the Minister's judgment (i.e., a ministerial pardon).

In T's case, a violation investigation based on (i) above took place on December 6, 2010 (five days after his sentencing) on the part of a Tokyo Immigration Control security officer. On May 23, 2012 (three months after he became an illegal overstayer), his violation in relation to (b) above was filed.

The violation inquiry took place on August 10, 2016, certifying and notifying him of the suspicion of violating Article 2-4 (i) and (b) of the Act. The Kanto Regional Parole Board decided two days later to grant T parole. Article 62 of the Immigration Control Act, "Furnishing of Information," regulates that regional parole boards, when granting release on parole to a foreigner serving a criminal sentence, shall report this information immediately. This duty of information is considered to ensure that upon parole, the Immigration Control Bureau can be sure to issue a detention or deportation order (*Article-by-Article Exegesis of the Immigration Control and Refugee Recognition Act: Fourth Edition,* p.930).

During the violation inquiry, while admitting that the facts were accurate, T refused to comply with this certification and demanded an oral inquiry. “I understood that if I obeyed the certification I would have to go back to Brazil. But I still want to stay in Japan, so I can’t obey it. Today I am here to request an oral inquiry” (Inquiry Record, August 10, 2016, p.16).

The oral inquiry judgment was made on August 31, 2016: “The immigration inspector’s certification of the suspect as the target of deportation is without error.” T lodged an objection on the same day. “Having received and understood the judgment notification, I refuse to obey the judgment and will lodge an objection.” (Oral Inquiry Record, August 31, 2016, p.13). T stated his reasons for the objection as follows. “I myself have lived in Japan since I was ten years old. I can hardly speak my mother tongue, and even if I can speak a little I can hardly understand it, so I couldn’t make a living in Brazil and I am uneasy about returning there. I am very frightened. My parents have lived in Japan for some twenty years, with hardly any family or acquaintances in Brazil. I would have no home and no work in Brazil. Please give me one last chance to make a life for myself in Japan. I will take it very seriously and work hard. I am really sorry about what I did. It is my dream to stay in Japan” (Appeal, August 31, 2016).

And yet, on September 13, 2016, the Tokyo Immigration Control Bureau Director judged that “the objection is invalid,” effectively confirming the deportation, and notified the Tokyo Senior Immigration Inspector thereof. This notification was issued [to T] on October 25: “You are hereby notified that a notification from the Tokyo Immigration Control Bureau Director has been received to the effect that your objection has been judged invalid.” The deportation order was issued on the same day.

Article 63-2 of the Immigration Control Act regulates with regard to the relation between issuing a deportation order and criminal procedures that “[i]n cases of a written deportation order having been issued pursuant to the provisions of the preceding paragraph, the enforcement of such order shall be carried out after the procedures pursuant to the provisions of laws and regulations related to criminal suits, enforcement of sentences or treatment of the inmates of juvenile homes or the women's guidance home have been completed. However, the enforcement of such order may be carried out with the approval of the Prosecutor-General or the Superintending Prosecutor even when the alien is still serving his/her sentence.” Let us confirm the meaning of this below in more detail.

In principle, the action of criminal justice and that of administration should be separate, without mutual interference. However, in real life, given that most reasons for deportation of foreigners are criminal cases and an individual being subject to a given penalty due to violation of the criminal code constitutes grounds for deportation, the two tend to collide. In particular, this collision of criminal justice and government action must be sorted out rationally when both are trying to realize their relative objectives by forcible restraint of the subject. The section detailed above regulates that the enforcement of a deportation order issued on a foreigner imprisoned due to the stipulations of laws such as criminal suits is to take place after the criminal proceedings have concluded and that the order may also be issued during the serving of their sentence with the permission of the Prosecutor-General or supervising prosecutor. This is considered a reasonable stipulation. In short, deportation proceedings, with the exception of detention and deportation itself, may move ahead during the subject's imprisonment on criminal proceedings, while the enforcement of deportation orders is also possible after the subject has been freed due to the end of their sentence, etc., if their continued restraint is ensured by the Immigration Control Bureau; this is because it is extremely difficult for the power of punishment to realize its effects once the subject has been deported out of the country (*Article-by-Article Exegesis of the Immigration Control and Refugee Recognition Act, Fourth Edition,* pp.933-937).

In T's case, the deportation order was issued on October 25, 2016, and enforced on October 27, 2016, via his detention in an immigration control facility, when the legal proceedings concerning his punishment were concluded due to the granting of parole. After he had fulfilled his criminal responsibility toward punishment under criminal law, he was immediately detained for deportation proceedings.

Summary

"My crimes got me in prison for seven years, but I worked hard and thought I would get out in six years and two months, ten months early, but unfortunately I was taken straight to immigration control without being let out, and it's been almost two years since then" (letter). According to T, he was informed of his parole just three days before the parole date. "Usually, when parole is granted, the parolee is informed a week or two in advance. T was probably not told until immediately beforehand because it was expected that he would be detained" (former Kanto Regional Parole Board coordination officer). T says that he was not told that he would be detained in an immigration facility on the day of his parole. "When they granted me parole, I thought my father and mother would come to meet me, but an Immigration Bureau staff member came instead and took me straight to the detention center."

Let us say that a foreigner who had committed serious crimes and been sentenced to twenty years in prison needed to renew their status of residence during their first year of imprisonment and that their application was refused. At this time, if the Prosecutor-General or supervising prosecutor granted permission for deportation proceedings and the foreigner in question returned to the country on the spot, most people would have a problem with the idea of permitting them to return without fulfilling their criminal responsibility. This kind of example makes it easy to understand the stance that restraint under criminal proceedings takes precedence, in principle, over deportation proceedings. Having committed a crime, fulfilling the responsibility therefor is a given. But criminal responsibility becomes meaningful only on the premise of rehabilitation thereafter. T served over four and a half years of his prison sentence as an illegal overstayer. How are we to understand the meaning of his time in prison, during which he remembers "working hard"? Prisons are said to have become places for "the rehabilitation and sound return to society of inmates," but in T's case, the rational arrangements made in the legal sense effectively represented nothing but sanctions.

Chapter 4

Suing the Authorities: What was Being Judged and How?

Suing the Authorities

Desperate to remain in Japan, on April 24, 2017, T lodged administrative litigation against the verdict which had not granted him special permission to remain, calling for the cancellation of the verdict and the deportation order based upon it, on grounds that it exceeded the scope of authority and represented illegal abuse of that authority. As the plaintiff, T demanded the following two points:

As the plaintiff, T demanded the following two points:

1. 1.Cancellation of the verdict of the Tokyo Immigration Control Bureau Director of September 13, 2016, judging the plaintiff's objection to be invalid, based on Article 49-1 of the Immigration Control and Refugee Recognition Act.
2. 1.Cancellation of the deportation order issued to the plaintiff by the Tokyo Immigration Bureau Control Senior Inspector on October 25, 2016.

T was defeated in both the Tokyo District Court and the Tokyo High Court. As the verdict of the High Court was essentially a confirmation of that of the District Court, the discussion here will focus on the arguments of the plaintiff, the defendant, and the court in the District Court. Trials appealing for the cancellation of a deportation order of this kind review not whether special permission to remain should have been granted to the plaintiff, but whether the defendant (the government and the Tokyo Immigration Control Bureau), in refusing to grant this permission, acted in excess and/or in abuse of their authority.

The Plaintiff's Arguments

The reasons for the suit included "The plaintiff has spent most of his life, including the formative period of his life, in Japan, all his family are in Japan, and cannot be considered reasonable to return him to the country of his nationality simply because formality calls for deportation" (Appeal, April 24, 2017, p.1). Regarding the illegality of the verdict in question, arguments were based on (1) the Guidelines for Special Permission to Stay (October 2006, revised July 2009) and (2) the clear excess and abuse of authority in terms of the principle of proportionality (ibid., p.3).

The Guidelines were prepared by the Ministry of Justice Immigration Control Bureau as items for consideration when judging whether to grant special permission to remain. In T's case, the plaintiff argued that the positive elements outweighed the negative elements: that is, that "the applicant has resided in Japan for a considerable period of time and is deemed to be settled in Japan" (among "Other positive elements") and the fact that if T were forced to return, his family would be decisively torn apart, constituted "humanitarian grounds or other special circumstances."

"The plaintiff came to live in Japan with his father, who is of Japanese heritage, and his mother, the spouse thereof, and has literally lived in Japan since childhood; he is still only 29, meaning that half his life, in particular the period of his growth to maturity from age 10 to the present, has been spent in Japan. All the plaintiff's family, that is his parents and younger brother, live in Japan and have no plans to return to Brazil; they are legally resident in Japan and have worked hard to build their lives here. If the plaintiff were to be forced to return to Brazil, it would tear his family decisively apart" (ibid., p.4). Regarding the negative elements, it was argued that while the breach of criminal law was by no means trivial, it should not be interpreted as a vicious or serious crime (as in the Guidelines' "Negative elements to be given particular consideration"), and criminal responsibility had already been fully carried out.

Regarding proportionality, the argument was that authority had been exceeded or abused because T was seriously disadvantaged by the verdict (the division of his family and the extreme difficulty of making a living in his country of origin) while the government would receive no particular advantages in protecting itself by refusing him permission to remain—that is, the disadvantages created by the verdict far outweighed its advantages. "If the plaintiff were to be deported to Brazil, he and his parents and brother would be separated and the family would be torn apart. In addition, the plaintiff would be forced to make a living without the support of his family in Brazil, where he had spent only his early childhood, and in realistic terms would have great difficulty building a stable life" (ibid., p.6).

In appeals for cancellation of deportation orders, the plaintiff generally argues that authority has been exceeded and abused from the perspective of the International Bill of Human Rights, related treaties, the Guidelines, and in terms of proportionality. In this case, the focus was particularly on the latter two.

The Defendant's Arguments

First, based on past Supreme Court verdicts (the October 1978 McLean trial, etc.), they confirmed that "legally, special permission to remain is essentially no more than a privilege granted to foreigners who are to be deported for admitted grounds, and application therefor on the part of the foreigners in question is not recognized" (Response, July 6, 2017, pp.12-13). Next, they argued that the specific requirements for special permission to stay are not indicated because the Minister of Justice is granted extremely wide authority. Because acts violating the immigration control system are severe offenses against national and social interests protected by law, it is considered appropriate to grant such wide authority to officials such as the Minister of Justice, when judging whether special permission to stay is consistent with the national interest of Japan. In addition, "because the Minister of Justice's authority on the judgment of special permission to remain is particularly qualitatively wide compared to that of the renewal of the status of residence of legally resident foreigners, it is difficult to conceive of a situation where that judgment could be considered an illegal excess or abuse of the Minister's authority" (ibid., pp.12-16).

They added two reasons to consider the verdict legally compliant. First, that the two deportation reasons of criminal law violation and illegal overstay applied to the plaintiff, who was thus clearly a foreigner who must be deported from Japan. Second, that there were no special circumstances deserving of special permission to remain, and that the plaintiff's status of residence was extremely malicious, as detailed in three additional points.

a. "It should be considered a major negative element that the plaintiff was sentenced to seven years' imprisonment for the crimes of robbery, breaking and entering, theft, and attempted robbery."

   Here, based on the public record of the trial leading to a criminal verdict, the plaintiff's ten crimes are listed in detail and deemed highly malicious. Regarding the plaintiff's argument that he has fully fulfilled his criminal responsibility, "as stated, the plaintiff's status of residence is highly malicious and cannot be ignored in terms of immigration control, an evaluation unchanged by his time in prison" (p.21).

b. "The plaintiff has committed many crimes and acts of delinquency during his residence in Japan, in addition to those indicated in a. above."

   Here the arguments touch on the plaintiff's multiple arrests for delinquency and sentences to probation in family court, the multiple sentences to protective custody thereafter leading to juvenile detention, and the second sentencing to juvenile detention, arguing in sum that even two opportunities for rehabilitation in juvenile detention were not enough and the plaintiff repeatedly committed crimes such as robbery as an adult, thus making his status of residence highly malicious.

c. "The plaintiff has illegally overstayed his period of residence."

Regarding the malice of the illegal overstay, "illegal overstay is in itself an act disturbing the order of the Japanese immigration control system and as such a criminal act of malice and a severe offense against national and social interests protected by law, so that regardless of its reasons or purposes, the fact of illegal overstay alone renders the plaintiff's status of residence malicious" (ibid., pp.22-23). As well, "as a result of being judged guilty of crimes in a court of law and being confined in prison, the plaintiff has overstayed his period of residence during his imprisonment, with thus no exceptional circumstances in the process of his overstay" (ibid., pp.22-23).

The following arguments are made regarding the plaintiff's settledness in Japan and difficulty making a living in his country of origin. Regarding settledness, as of his 19 years resident in Japan, it was argued that the plaintiff had spent almost nine of them in juvenile detention or prison, and committed many crimes during his ten years of freedom as well, "he is not recognized as settled into general society" (ibid., p.24). In addition, "regarding the judgment on special permission to stay, the Immigration Control Act does not regulate that consideration is required for the foreigner's family relations, lifestyle basis in his country of origin, capacity in his mother tongue, or other specific items" (ibid., p.25). It was further argued that, given that the plaintiff was studying his mother tongue and was a young and healthy adult male, and that there were no specific circumstances preventing the plaintiff and his family from engaging in mutual economic support, he should be able to make a living in his country of origin, and that it should be considered that "even if he suffers from disadvantages upon deportation to his country of origin, it is essentially a situation which he has brought upon himself."

Based on the above, the argument is that "the plaintiff's arguments are not deserving of special consideration with regard to the granting of special permission to remain." With regard to the Guidelines, the stance is that they are not criteria for special permission to remain but only examples of possible consideration when determining whether to grant such permission. With regard to proportionality, it was argued that the judgment of the Minister of Justice on the granting of special permission to remain is not bound by the principle of proportionality.

4 The Tokyo District Court Verdict

The Tokyo District Court handed down its verdict on January 25, 2018 (suit for cancellation of deportation order). The verdict was a defeat for the plaintiff: "1. The plaintiff's requests are all dismissed. 2. The court costs are to be covered by the plaintiff."

The reason given for the verdict was that the defense arguments were accepted across the board. Because the Minister of Justice is given extremely wide authority regarding the judgment on special permission to remain, that judgment can be illegal only when it entirely lacks a factual basis or is highly inappropriate in terms of social principles. Regarding the Guidelines, they are considered as sample categories of items which are considered for the judgment in question into positive and negative elements. Four other points were discussed, concerning the plaintiff's status of entry and residence, his relations with his family remaining in Japan, his degree of settledness in Japan, and his life to be made in his country of origin.

His status of residence was considered highly malicious due to the heavy sentence of seven years' imprisonment with labor, as well as multiple counts of delinquency (there was no specific reference to illegal overstay), with no special circumstances worthy of consideration for judgment. Regarding family relations, given that the plaintiff had lived separately from his parents and brother at one point, no special need to care for or financially support them was recognized. Regarding settledness, it was argued that the plaintiff had spent long periods in juvenile detention and prison, and had not led a stable life elsewhere either. Regarding life in his country of origin, based on his capacity in his mother tongue, youth, health, and cooperative relations with relatives in Brazil, it was argued repeatedly that "it is unlikely that he will have serious problems making a living in Brazil."

The verdict thus stated that "the plaintiff's residence in Japan has been extremely malicious, marked by multiple criminal acts, which should be considered as major negative elements: neither is special consideration required with regard to his relations with his family remaining in Japan, his degree of settledness in Japan, his difficulty making a living in his country of origin, etc. Therefore, the judgment not to grant the plaintiff special permission to stay is not recognized as having lacked a factual basis or run seriously counter to social principles, thus not constituting an excess or abuse of the authority vested in the Tokyo Immigration Control Bureau Director" (Verdict, January 25, 2018, pp.20-21). In addition, based on the judgment above, it was judged that the principle of proportionality could not be adopted.

Arguments

(1) Perspective on the background of delinquency and crime

With regard to the plaintiff's crimes (factual violations of criminal law), the plaintiff argued that while not minor, they were not vicious or serious (negative elements to be given particular consideration under the Guidelines), while the defense argued that they were serious negative elements. The District Court also saw them as serious negative elements, and judged that the plaintiff's status of residence was highly malicious. Common to both arguments was the absence of any reference to the background or specific circumstances leading the plaintiff to commit delinquency and crimes, with only a direct reference to motivation in the court verdict: “The plaintiff was in need of money for daily life and leisure, and turned thoughtlessly to crime” (Verdict, January 25, 2018, p.15). However, when debating the malice and criminal severity of a criminal act, it is natural to consider the background and reasons behind individual cases. In T’s case, the background of his school non-attendance and subsequent delinquency involved various factors: the lack of any special support for students needing Japanese instruction, communication capacity, inability to make friends, being bullied, the absence of a place to learn or feel at home, inability to refuse invitations from bad friends, and so on. The court failed entirely to address any of these factors which drove T to leave school and fall into delinquency.

(2) Criminal responsibility

While the plaintiff argued that he had sufficiently fulfilled his criminal responsibility, the defense argued that the fact of his time in prison did not change the evaluation (that his status of residence was malicious). The verdict likewise judged that “having been granted parole does not affect the judgment of the plaintiff’s malicious status of residence” (Verdict, January 25, 2018, p.18). According to the logic of the defense and the verdict, in terms of effect on the judgment of malice, no matter how much effort the plaintiff was to put in toward rehabilitation, it would mean nothing.

On this point, the plaintiff argued that "given that foreigners who have committed crimes are considered undesirable for the nation, the facts of having atoned for his crime, undergone education and training for rehabilitation, and been paroled before the end of his sentence should be considered in the judgment of the plaintiff's antisociality and whether he is undesirable for the nation as well; these facts should be understood as reducing the plaintiff's antisociality" (First Prepared Document, August 30, 2017, p.3). If a foreigner is designated undesirable for the nation based on having committed an act of malice, the degree of amendment to this designation based on their work toward rehabilitation in prison should also be considered. However, this argument went entirely unaddressed in the verdict. The facts of the background to the criminal act and the work toward rehabilitation while serving a sentence were left out of the discussion, with only malice addressed, on the absolutist basis of having committed a crime and been sentenced to prison.

(3) The malice of illegal overstay

T became an illegal overstayer during his time in prison, when his application for renewal of his status as a long-term resident was rejected. As a prisoner, he was unable to leave the country. Regardless of these circumstances, the defense argued that "regardless of its reasons or purposes, the fact of illegal overstay alone renders the plaintiff's status of residence malicious." Assigning malice regardless of reasons or purposes, looking at the fact of illegal overstaying alone, bears resemblance to the attitude taken by the courts towards his delinquency and crimes.

On this point, the plaintiff responded to the defense's view above with "While the plaintiff applied for renewal of his status of residence before the period of residence granted was over, his application was rejected and he was unable to leave the country due to being in prison at the time (if anything, he was responsible for completing his prison term in Japan), so that, given the specifics which led to his period of residence passing, the fact that it did so cannot be called a 'malicious act disturbing the order of the immigration control system and a severe offense against national and social interests protected by law'" (First Prepared Document, August 30, 2017, pp.3-4); however, this point was not addressed.

Probably, there was almost no chance that applications for renewal of status of residence would be accepted when coming from someone like T, sentenced at the time to imprisonment with or without labor for life or a period exceeding one year. At that stage, the foreigner has effectively lost any chance to try again in Japan: even after fulfilling his criminal responsibility, deportation as an illegal overstayer awaits him. His Japanese counterpart is given a chance to try again if he works for rehabilitation and fulfills his criminal responsibility, but the foreigner's situation is completely different. The difference in nationality imposes a terrible inequality.

(4) Settledness, family, life in the country of origin

T came to Japan at the age of ten and lived there for some twenty years thereafter, but almost half of that time was spent in juvenile detention and prison. The defense argued that he could not be recognized as having settled into ordinary society, based on the length of his detention and his repeated criminal acts during the remainder of his time in Japan. On this point, the plaintiff argued that "juvenile detention and prisons are systems and facilities established in Japanese society, which conduct education and training expressly intended for independence and rehabilitation in Japanese society, so it is wrong to consider that the period of detention was spent separated from Japanese society" (First Prepared Document, August 30, 2017, p.4). The verdict adopted an interpretation wholly accepting the defense's argument.

It is decisive that, if T were deported, his family would be sundered. His sentence to seven years' imprisonment was extremely serious, given that grounds for refusal of entry begin at a year or more in prison. There was almost no chance that T would be able to return to Japan. T's family might be able to travel to Brazil to see him. The defense argued, in fact, that “they [author’s note: the plaintiff’s father, mother, and brother] are understood to be able to travel to Brazil to see the plaintiff, so that deportation to his country of origin would not necessarily mean permanent separation from his family in Japan” (Response, July 6, 2017, p.26). However, T and his parents and brother would clearly find life as a family extremely difficult.

Another problem in the event of deportation would be the possibility or difficulty of making a living in Brazil. What happens when someone who came to Japan at age ten and spent twenty years there returns suddenly to a country where he has no basis for his living? While able to converse in his mother tongue to some extent, with no academic background and no one to rely on, the reality awaiting him would inevitably be harsh in the extreme.

Summary

The lawyer Koichi Kodama points out that because being the target of deportation means being deprived of physical freedom and the basis of daily life, thus driven into extremely harsh circumstances, many people sue to have the denial of special permission to remain retracted, and yet very few of these suits succeed; he also summarizes these cases. The major factor in the scarcity of successful suits, he says, is that the courts have an extremely limited interpretation of the circumstances in which the authority of the Minister of Justice could be exceeded or abused. In addition, the overall tendency in successful cases is notably affected by whether the severity of the facts is accepted, rather than a focus on interpretation of the breadth of authority (Kodama, 2010).

Shin'ichiro Nakajima, an NGO representative, considers the almost nonexistent successful suits in administrative litigations concerning immigration control, particularly suits for cancellation of deportation orders, to be a problem, calling them "the closed door." According to Nakajima, foreign plaintiffs lodging administrative litigation related to deportation proceedings fall into six categories: (1) people whose applications for refugee certification have been refused; (2) families of Japanese war orphans in China who are not blood relations (adopted children, pre-marriage children), whose entry rights have been cancelled for posing as their actual children; (3) foreign spouses of Japanese with no residence status who submitted their marriage documents after detection/arrest; (4) overstaying families with children; (5) overstaying couples both of foreign nationality with no children; (6) single overstaying foreigners. However, in the cases of (5) and (6), while it is logically possible, realistically they "cannot expect to receive special permission to remain," and administrative litigation is extremely rare, with no instances of relief measures via successful litigation (Nakajima, 2010, p.147).

T lodged his suit as a single foreigner. Based on the existing trends in suits requesting the cancellation of deportation orders and the fact of his seven years in prison, he faced extremely harsh conditions in doing so.

Chapter 5

Long-Term Detention and the Provisional Release System

Daily Life in Immigration Control Facilities

Foreigners are detained on the basis of a detention or deportation order. Detention orders indicate detention up to 60 days, while deportation orders enable long-term detention with no maximum. T was detained at the Shinagawa Immigration Control Bureau on October 27, 2016, and transferred to the Higashi-Nihon Immigration Center on March 10, 2017. His period of detention (as of June 2019) has already exceeded two and a half years.

Detention centers are facilities for deportation and, unlike juvenile detention centers or prisons, offer no corrective education or rehabilitative programs. According to "Questions for the Higashi-Nihon Immigration Center" (October 13, 2016), the detainees' schedule, governed by the regulations for treatment, is as follows. "7:00: get up; 7:30: cleaning; 8:00: breakfast, 8:40: morning roll call; 11:30: lunch, 16:30: dinner, 17:00: evening roll call, 22:00: bed. Room doors are opened twice a day (8:40 to 11:30 and 13:30 to 17:00). Telephone calls, laundry, and showers are permitted. Exercise in the outdoor exercise area is possible for 40 minutes a day." Each floor contains its own block, where the detainees spend the majority of their time; the times when doors are open and free movement around the block is possible are limited, as noted above, and detainees essentially spend the remaining time in their rooms.

T spends his time in his room reading (Japanese novels), studying (mainly Japanese), watching television, listening to music, and so on. However, he says that the prison-like life causes significant stress. Because the Center is prone to various issues, he sticks to reading in order to avoid becoming involved. He recounts that many people become ill, struggle with insomnia, and take large quantities of medication. T says "Outside Japan, I don't think people are ever detained for this long. It's only Japan that shuts us up for so long and won't let us out. It's prison." Here is T's account (partially corrected) of one day in a week in April 2019.

○ April 15, 2019 (Monday)

Today I got up around 7:00, ate breakfast at 8:00, and went to morning roll call around 8:30. From about 9:20 free time began so I went outside. I charged my razor battery and shaved. There's a form you have to write called an application for luggage organization, so I wrote it. Then I had nothing else to do, so I greeted everyone and went back to my room to watch a movie. That was the morning. I ate lunch around 11:40 and then we had free time again from 13:00, but my room is the only one that has cleaning from 13:00. Afterward I had coffee. From 13:55 to about 14:35 was exercise time and we played soccer for 50 minutes. Today we won nine to one. After exercise and taking a shower, there was a letter from Professor Matsuo Tamaki that I got. Free time lasted until about 17:10, so that was it for the day. We had evening roll call at 17:45 and I finished dinner at 18:00 and then watched a movie. From 19:00 I watched TV, and at 22:00 I went to bed.

Taesung Go has called foreigner detention facilities, where no education or training for rehabilitation is provided, spaces like "controlled waiting rooms for excluded foreigners" (Go, 2016-2017, p.36).

The Background to Long-Term Detention

T's period of detention at the Higashi-Nihon Immigration Center alone has already exceeded two years. Generally, anything over six months is considered long-term detention. According to "Questions for the Higashi-Nihon Immigration Center" (above), the breakdown of detainees' time there is as follows: of 253 detainees, 125 (49.4%) have been there for "one day to less than three months," 47 (18.6%) for "three months to less than six months," 70 (27.7%) for "six months to less than one year," 5 (2.0%) for "one year to less than eighteen months," 4 (1.6%) for "eighteen months to less than two years," and 2 (0.8%) for "two years or more." Long-term detainees (six months or more) comprise 32%, and those detained for two years or more just 0.8% of the whole. However, the number of long-term detainees has shot up since 2017.

According to the Ministry of Justice, the total number of detainees over the six years from 2013 to 2018, the number of long-term detainees (continuous detention of six months or more), and the percentage of the latter among the whole has shifted as follows. Total detainee numbers have been 914 in 2013, 932 in 2014, 1,003 in 2015, 1,133 in 2016, 1,351 in 2017, and 2,018 in 2018. Long-term detainee numbers have been respectively 263, 290, 290, 313, 576, and 704, accounting for 28.8%, 31.1%, 28.9%, 27.6%, 42.6%, and 34.9% of the whole. While the number of detainees as a whole has increased consistently, there has been a notable increase in the numbers of long-term detainees since 2017 and their percentages of the whole.

According to a pamphlet of the Association Concerned with Issues at Ushiku Migrant Detention Center, as of the end of December 2018, of the 325 detainees at the Higashi-Nihon Immigration Center, 306 were long-term detainees of six months or more, accounting for 92.4% of the whole. Nine out of ten detainees were long-term detainees.

The basic reason for long-term detention is that there is no legal limit on the detention period. On this point, Article 52-5 of the Immigration Control Act states that "if a foreign national cannot be deported immediately, the immigration control officer may detain him/her in an immigration detention center, detention house, or any other place designated by the Minister of Justice or by the supervising immigration inspector commissioned by the Minister of Justice until such time as deportation becomes possible." In addition, when considering the background and issues of long-term detention, we must bear in mind the fact that most foreigners issued with deportation orders leave Japan at their own expense. The data on deportation orders issued and persons deported in recent years indicates that over 90% of the 6,000 to 7,000 people issued yearly with deportation orders return at their own expense to their countries of origin. Flights for group deportation were sometimes chartered in the past, but forcible deportation, including these methods, has been frequently considered problematic from both humanitarian and cost (tax) viewpoints. The basic policy of the Ministry of Justice is to encourage foreigners to return to their countries of origin at their own expense. Therefore, if the person in question refuses to leave, their deportation can be delayed.

Reasons for the increase in long-term detainees cited by the Ministry of Justice include "refusal to accept the detainee by their country of origin" (the embassy in Japan of the country of origin refuses to issue a temporary passport for deportation evaders), "abusive application for refugee status" (abuse of the refugee application system on the grounds that an application in process will halt deportation proceedings), and "litigation against the authorities (suit for cancellation)" (based on the right to undergo trial, actual deportation proceedings against the plaintiff are halted until the trial is complete). The Ministry of Justice considers as problematic the increased medical costs and issues with maintaining order in facilities caused by long-term detention. The latter involves increased risks such as detainees going on hunger strikes for provisional release, verbal and physical assaults on staff, feigned illness and general malaise, and group demonstrations (MOJ *Deportation Duties* 2018, 2019).

The Provisional Release System

Apart from leaving Japan, the only way to be freed from these detention centers is provisional release. Permission for provisional release is granted or refused based on an overall judgment of the issues in each individual case, upon application. There are no criteria for permission, but items for consideration are as follows: the reason for charges or deportation, the reason for the request for provisional release and its evidence, the detainee's character, age, assets, behavior, state of health, family situation, and length of detention, the would-be guarantor's age, occupation, income, assets, behavior, relation to the detainee and willingness to receive them, the risks of absconding or violation of provisional release conditions, the influence on national benefits or security, the possible risk of human trafficking, etc., and other special circumstances.

Even if the detainee is granted provisional release and permitted to leave the center, they are not exempt from redetention and deportation; further, while on provisional release they are under strict restrictions such as prohibitions on work, movement to places (prefectures) not requested in advance and so on (Go, 2016-2017, p.38).

The Immigration Control Bureau explains the prohibition on work as follows: "Persons who have been issued with a deportation order are to be deported, as their residence in Japan is not permitted. Based on the need to keep them in custody and to prohibit activities of residence in Japan until their deportation, they are detained in a national or regional immigration detention center. Even if they are temporarily released from custody on the basis of provisional release, they have still been issued with a deportation order, and may not engage in work."

On September 18, 2015, the Director of the Ministry of Justice Immigration Control Bureau issued a Notice entitled "Appropriate Operation and Monitoring Concerned with Provisional Release Measures for Detainees Under Deportation Orders," specifying stricter measures to be taken against provisional releasees and detainees. From October 1, immediately thereafter, all immigration detention centers added a prohibition against work to their provisional release permits. Until that time, Immigration Control had tacitly overlooked provisional releasees' employment, but this Notice made its prohibition clear in writing (Provisional Release Association in Japan (PRAJ), "What is Immigration Control's Purpose in Long-Term Detention?").

Further, on April 7, 2016, the Director of the Ministry of Justice Immigration Control Bureau sent a notification to the directors of national and regional immigration detention centers entitled "Approaches Toward a Safe and Secure Society." With reference to the Tokyo Olympics and Paralympics scheduled for 2020, this notice read "To realize a safe and secure society, one important element is ensuring domestic security; urgent issues for this Bureau, along with smooth immigration inspections, strict border measures, and suitable refugee certification inspections, include significant reductions in the number of illegal overstayers and false residents, who have been on the increase in recent years, as well as in foreigners posing concern to Japanese society, such as those issued with deportation orders who have avoided deportation." Thus, people avoiding deportation are positioned as a threat to Japanese society. Because it is the only way to get out of the center, T has applied for provisional release seven times so far. The first six times were all refused; as of July 2019, he is in the process of his seventh application.

Let us look at the center's total number of applications and the rates of permission granted. According to "Questions for the Higashi-Nihon Immigration Center," there were 1,025 applications in 2013 (309 accepted to 713 rejected), 866 in 2014 (281 to 582), 818 in 2015 (351 to 464), and 488 in 2016 (195 to 156). With "others withdrawn," the number of applications and the number of the total of accepted and rejected applications do not match. Allowing for this, if we look at the percentages of permission granted, they are 30.1% in 2013, 32.4% in 2014, 42.9% in 2015, and 40.0% in 2016.

Because the process of provisional release application inspection and the reasons for refusal are a black box, the precise reasons are unknown, but it is thought that in T's case his prison sentence for robbery is the major obstacle. In addition, the Director of the Ministry of Justice Immigration Control Bureau has issued numerous notices and directions reinforcing the stringency of the immigration control system, including provisional release ("Appropriate Operation and Monitoring Concerned with Provisional Release Measures for Detainees Under Deportation Orders" of September 18, 2015; "Thorough Reinforcement of 'Appropriate Operation' and 'Monitoring' in the Notice of the Previous Year (Directions)" of September 28, 2016; "Further Thorough Reinforcement of Suitable Operation and Monitoring of Provisional Release for Persons Issued with Deportation Orders" (February 28, 2018), etc.). Upon a request for information release issued by a lawyers' group, the documents released as of February 28, 2018 noted the provisional release operation policy thus: "Persons deemed unsuitable for provisional release, even those with no deportation schedule, are to be continuously detained to the extent possible until deportation becomes possible, except for those too seriously unwell for detention." The list includes "those punished for serious antisocial crimes posing concern to society, such as murder, robbery, human trafficking, bribery, drug offense, etc."

One lawyer remarks that "essentially, except for cases of serious illness, once you are in detention you're not coming out again. Their plan is to keep you in until you give in and then send you back to your country. No other developed country has a system like this." According to detainee supporters and lawyers encountered at the Higashi-Nihon Immigration Center, provisional release has become much harder to obtain over the last year, probably due, in one lawyer's opinion, to the upcoming Tokyo Olympics.

The number of provisional releasees on deportation orders peaked in 2015 at 3,606 people, thereafter decreasing: 3,555 in 2016, 3,106 in 2017, and 2,796 in 2018 (as of June) (Ministry of Justice, above, p.1). A look at the average number of days required to process an application for provisional release shows an increase: for each year from 2013, 46 days, 56 days, 51 days, and 69 days. Application processing times have in some cases risen to over 100 days, and the longest times for each year have been 176 days, 205 days, 113 days, and 120 days.

T has refused deportation on the grounds that he wants to live with his family resident in Japan, he wants to go back to school in Japan, he will not be able to make a life in his country of origin, and so on. He has also repeatedly applied for provisional release. By this point, the Higashi-Nihon Immigration Center is now almost entirely populated with people like T, long-term detainees living with indefinite detention and the anxiety of possible forcible deportation at any time.

The Contamination Incident

Article 61-7.3 of the Immigration Control Act regulates, with regard to the treatment of detainees, that “the supplies furnished to the detainee shall be adequate and the accommodation of the immigration detention center shall be maintained in sanitary conditions.” “Supplies” here refers to food and other materials.

On May 8, 2019, the Higashi-Nihon Immigration Center Treatment Division Group 1 Immigration Security Chief submitted a "Report on Contamination in Official Meals" to the Director of the Center ("Decision to Disclose Personal Information Held (Notice)," June 5, 2019). The report described the incident as follows. "On May 8 of this year at XX:XX, the interphone from Room 205, Dorm 2 rang and T [his full name] requested my presence. When I arrived at his room, he showed me the dessert container provided, in which I found a dead insect about 1 mm in diameter attached to the pineapple offered for dessert. I reported the situation to Deputy Governor XX.

Measures after the fact: (1) At XX:XX, I provided an alternate meal for the detainee, who received it with thanks. (2) At XX:XX, when patrolling the B side of Dorm 2, T called me in and showed me the alternate meal provided, in which I found a hair about 3 mm long attached to the spaghetti. I reported this to Deputy Governor XX. T said that he did not need another alternate meal, as it was late and he no longer wanted to eat, and asked us to take greater care. I told him that care would be taken to prevent a recurrence and collected the meal containers. (3) XX." (XX refers to blacked-out portions).

"I want to tell you something. On May 8, 2019, Thursday, there were three insect incidents. I think you can tell from just one meal how badly they treat the detainees and how they discriminate against us. Immigration Control and the Ministry of Justice are violating the law. I think they're supposed to inspect the meals, but they don't. If they inspected the meals properly, there wouldn't be bugs in the food. Article 27 says that the Director, etc. must inspect the food supplied to detainees. It's a violation. We just want to eat our meals with peace of mind, but Immigration Control won't even let us do that. A lot of people here have eating disorders or don't want to eat now. I'm sorry this letter is so hard to read, but thank you for reading." (letter)

With reference to meals, a correctional education officer at a juvenile detention made a memorable comment while showing me the lunch in the kitchen during a tour of the facility. "For the youths [in detention], meals are the only thing they have to look forward to. We try very hard to make sure the hot foods are hot, the cold foods are cold, and so on." Article 27 of the Regulations on Treatment of Detainees says that "food supplied to detainees shall be inspected." This contamination incident was not exceptional. At the Higashi-Nihon Immigration Center alone, with regard to meals served to detainees being contaminated by hairs, etc., there were 40 incidents in 2016, 60 in 2017, and 80 in the first six months of 2018, showing a steady increase (*Ehime Shimbun*, September 24, 2018).

Summary

Juvenile detention has treatment periods and prison has sentences, but there is no legal limit to the period of detention in immigration facilities. The Immigration Control Act states that the detainee may be detained "until such time as deportation becomes possible." In addition, while the sentencing of delinquent youths to juvenile detention and of criminals to prison takes place through the judgment and verdicts of the courts, there is no system for legal inquiry built into the judgment process of detention, and so Immigration Control makes its own judgments detaining those issued with deportation orders in immigration facilities. The only thing required to detain foreigners in this category is a detention order issued by an Immigration Control inspector, with the detention period likewise determined by Immigration Control. When a detainee applies for provisional release, neither the detainee nor their lawyer is privy to the inspection process, and no specific reasons are given when permission is refused.

In general, when placed in a wretched environment with absolutely no way of knowing when they will be able to leave it behind, people become increasingly prone to despair. The Association Concerned with Issues at Ushiku Migrant Detention Center told the press on July 24, 2019, that some 100 detainees at the Higashi-Nihon Immigration Center were holding a hunger strike in protest of long-term detention.

Chapter 6

Discussion and Conclusion

The Failure to Accept People of Japanese Descent

In May 2006, the Deputy Minister of Justice, serving as chair of a Ministry project team discussing immigration reform, gave a press conference introducing a proposal for drastic reform of the current system (in which workers of Japanese heritage are accepted as long-term residents), mentioning issues with the education of their children and saying "Japanese society has lacked the intent and the drive to accept overseas Japanese, seeing them only as labor. We need to admit to our failure and try again." From April 2006, the Ministry of Justice made it compulsory for long-term residents applying for visa renewal to add a certificate of criminal innocence, in addition to the "good behavior" item listed among the status qualifications. Part of the background for this changing system was the increase in South American-born criminals. Brazilians were the second most frequently arrested after Chinese, with Peruvians being sixth (in order, China, Brazil, Vietnam, South Korea, the Philippines, and Peru).

The MOJ Research and Training Institute also noted the following in an appendix to its investigative report on juvenile detention centers nationwide of 2010. "With regard to the children coming to Japan as long-term residents in the early 1990s in particular, they suffered from severely insufficient Japanese language education and school acceptance systems, in some cases reaching adulthood without sufficient opportunities to master Japanese and learn how to live in Japanese society. A certain number of these youths became delinquent and, in young adulthood, criminal; with concerns that they may become hardened repeat offenders, in order to prevent this situation from arising, it appears necessary to implement the rapid adoption of various measures listed above and treatment of long-term resident foreigners making full use of relevant policies” (Research and Training Institute, 2013, p.139).

To some extent, governmental personnel share the awareness that various problems have been caused by the acceptance of individuals of Japanese descent without sufficiently designed systems in place. Early on, it was thought that they would find it easy to adapt to Japanese society and that they would return in a few years to their countries of origin. There was no expectation of children coming to Japan. Therefore, there was almost no view on the need for education of children of Japanese descent. While many of them did come to Japan with the initial intent of returning in a few years, in most cases, they became long-term residents, with the number of foreign children increasing as more people summoned their families to Japan or arrived with their families.

The reality that perhaps most strikingly draws attention to the governmental failure is the increase of delinquency and crime among children with Japanese heritage. Its ultimate cause, as in the statement above, is the failure to see people with Japanese heritage as anything but labor and the lack of intent and drive to accept them as residents in Japan and as human beings. Having discussed the reality of T’s twenty years in Japan and the factors that have defined it above, this chapter will clarify any particularly notable points of argument.

“Long-Term Resident” as a Status of Residence

T was brought to Japan by his parents at age ten. The fact of the family having moved together can be explained by the Japanese government’s policies on the acceptance of foreign workers. Global economic inequities form overall push and pull factors in the international movement of labor, which the accepting countries heavily regulate through their immigration control systems, specifically the scale of influx and its attributes.

Factors in the policies encouraging T’s family to enter Japan included the establishment of qualifications for the status or position of a long-term resident under the 1989 revised Immigration Control and Refugee Recognition Act. The status of long-term resident applies to “those who are authorized to reside in Japan with a designation of period of stay by the Minister of Justice in consideration of special circumstances.” Periods of stay may be five years, three years, one year, or six months. Long-term residents are divided into notification long-term residents, who correspond to the conditions notified in advance by the Minister of Japan, and other non-notification long-term residents. Those to whom the former applies include foreigners of second- or third-generation Japanese ethnicity. T’s family, all of Japanese heritage, entered Japan in 1998 with long-term resident status.

It is well known that the long-term resident status was established in order to eliminate labor shortages. It did in fact serve to encourage South Americans of Japanese descent to come to Japan as temporary workers. Because the long-term resident qualifications relate to status or location, residents have freedom of movement and employment within Japan. Movement across borders of family units often takes place when the worker moves alone and, having achieved a certain standard of living, summons their family to join them. T's father most likely chose to bring T and his mother along on his return to Japan because, having worked there for three years, he was prepared to some extent to make a life in Japan.

Generally, the governments of the host countries prefer foreign workers who will contribute to the country's economic growth as short-term low-paid labor. In order not to incur various costs and risks, they accept foreigners on the premise that their stay will be temporary and for work purposes, rather than as migrants with long-term residence in mind, and control them stringently. The Japanese government's Technical Intern Training Program, used to bring in foreign labor, sharply reflects this mindset. This system does not permit trainees to change their place of employment (or training) or bring their families, returning them to their countries after just one to three years.

These three conditions for the Technical Intern Training Program condemn working foreigners to extremely harsh working and living environments. When compelled to work in poor training or employment environments, their choices are to put up with it or escape. Families are divided by the rule against bringing family members to Japan. Workers must return to their countries even if they have not accomplished their economic objectives. Those who borrowed money for the travel costs are particularly affected by the short-term employment.

Unlike the strictly controlled trainees, long-term residents of Japanese heritage have the freedom to choose their work, bring their families, and summon their children. However, while making it easy to bring children to Japan, this freedom also plunges the children into difficult situations. Thrown into a different culture where they do not even speak the language, it should be no surprise that they may find themselves maladapting without special consideration and support. One of these children, who became a student of mine in the School of International Studies at Utsunomiya University, recalls that she despaired upon first coming to Japan: “I thought I couldn’t survive in this place where I couldn’t read anything and I couldn’t speak the language.” She says that she was lucky to find herself in a good environment where everyone around her was kind.

Most South Americans of Japanese descent who have come to Japan as long-term residents for work are thought to have planned to return to their countries of origin in a few years. The author’s research on Peruvians with over twenty years in Japan found that hardly any of them initially planned to stay in Japan long term (Tamaki et al., 2014). However, while living in Japan, they gradually developed the intent to remain, based on factors including the status of family adaptation, their children's growth, the unstable economic and political states of their countries of origin, the higher standard of living in Japan, and so on. In particular, as children adapt to life in Japan, the orientation to long-term residency is enhanced through the desire to take good care of the children, raise them in a good environment, and see them well educated.

T's family likewise originally planned to stay only a few years. However, seeing T come home happy from elementary school, their orientation gradually shifted from returning to staying. And yet T's lifestyle and behavior changed dramatically after he entered junior high school, when he stopped attending school and fell into delinquency and crime. In the end he was to spend much of his life in Japan behind bars in juvenile detention, prison, and immigration facilities. Eventually, the family was torn apart. T's family remains helplessly divided.

The fundamental cause of this reality is the misalignment between policy that has designed a system easily enabling overseas Japanese workers and their children to come to Japan, without properly taking account of their longer-term residency and the increasing number of such children, and policy that has failed to create a system able to handle children flung into a different cultural environment. The disadvantage at which foreign children are placed is related to the general shortage of ethnic social capital in Japan (Higuchi & Inaba,

2018).

For example, in the United States, with its large-scale immigration and tendency for immigrants to live in specific areas, second-generation immigrants often tend to have many friends within the immigrant community. In Japan, however, second-generation immigrants find themselves in classrooms almost completely made up of Japanese children. According to the composition of schools with foreign students requiring Japanese language instruction (MEXT "Survey on Acceptance Status of Students Requiring Japanese Language Instruction," 2016 results), among elementary schools, 37.6% had one such student, 19.8% had two, 10.1% had three, and 6.6% had four, while among junior high schools, 48.0% had one, 18.3% had two, 8.6% had three, and 4.9% had four. Elementary schools with four or fewer foreign children make up 74.1% of the whole; in the case of junior high schools, 79.8%. If the status of long-term residence had not been created, T's father would not have come to Japan, and thus T would not have done so either.

The Background to Recidivism: Based on the Research and Training Institute Report

T's first stumble came a few months after entering junior high school, when he stopped attending school. His second was when truancy led to delinquency, and his third when he reverted to delinquency a few months after his parole from the first juvenile detention center.

When considering the issue of recidivism in delinquency, the results of the MOJ Research and Training Institute surveys are extremely helpful. The Institute conducted a survey of 90 young people with foreign citizenship (excluding Special Permanent Residents) or with Japanese citizenship but limited Japanese-language abilities, thus requiring consideration different from Japanese young people, who were detained or newly admitted into juvenile detention centers throughout Japan from June 1 through November 30, 2010.

The number of delinquent foreign young people in juvenile detention increased from 1996 through 2003, peaking at 104 in 2003 before declining again. Of those judged as foreigners, etc., requiring treatment different from Japanese and receiving such treatment, 70 to 90% were of Brazilian nationality through 2008, but recently this group is becoming more diverse in nationality. The report presents several of the 31 case studies of daily life and treatment during probation; here I quote one particularly similar to T's case and another in contrast thereto.

Case study 1: Repeat delinquency through renewed contact with badly behaved friends (pp.73-74)

The young person is a South American-Japanese born in Japan who attended a school for foreigners through early elementary school but, due to high fees, transferred to public school in fourth grade. After entering junior high school he began to spend time with his accomplices (Japanese) and was taken into protective custody for late-night misbehavior, etc., leading to his expulsion from school. His parents, focused on their work, were unable to supervise him appropriately, and in the course of delinquency with his badly behaved friends, he committed mugging with violence [so-called "*oyaji* hunting" targeting middle-aged and older men] and was sentenced to juvenile detention.

While born in Japan, he began to study Japanese formally only after transferring to a public elementary school, and upon entering juvenile detention could read and write only at a lower elementary level. He acquired Japanese ability sufficient to write proper characters in a letter to a probation officer. He received his junior high school diploma while in detention. Because his parents spoke little Japanese, during the environmental preparation before his parole, the probation officer explained the system to his parents and discussed his life after parole with the aid of documents in their native language and an interpreter.

Special conditions for his parole included the prohibition of contact with his accomplices and of wandering around at night; on this basis, he returned to his parents' home for probation. While he hoped to enter high school and after his parole worked part-time jobs while studying for high school entrance, after some time he was admonished for receiving contact from his badly behaved friends. When the probation officer confirmed his status with his mother on a visit, she said that she didn't know how he was doing as he was working at night. Although hoping to enter a credit-based high school while working, he was unable to pass the entrance exam. Under these conditions, bragging about delinquency at the home of a delinquent friend escalated into a repeat of the mugging incident along with two Japanese friends, leading to their arrest. His probation was canceled due to this repeat delinquency and he was once again sentenced to juvenile detention.

Case study 2: Release granted due to high school acceptance after attending a local tutoring school while continuing employment (pp.72-73)

With South American parents of Japanese descent, the young person was born in Japan and has never lived in his country of origin. His parents are separated and his home environment is poor (with siblings likewise sentenced to juvenile detention for delinquency). After entering junior high school, he fell into bad company and began delinquent behavior such as motorcycle theft and shoplifting, being sentenced to juvenile detention for theft. Given that his home environment was poor and his mother unable to supervise him, the family court called for measures to be taken from early on to arrange possible alternate housing for him after juvenile detention in order to enable rehabilitation.

As a result of discussions and arrangements with his mother after he had started detention in the process of preparing living arrangements for him, his mother decided to move house before he was paroled in order to improve his friendships, enabling her house him after his detention. Special conditions including continued work and the prohibition of contact with his accomplices were set, and he was paroled from detention to his mother's new home for probation.

Probation measures included the objective of establishing future goals through finding work immediately and remaining employed as well as enrolling in a part-time high school. The young person began work immediately after his parole at an automotive company. As he hoped to enter high school, he began to attend the basic academic tutoring offered by a local NPO in order to prepare for the entrance exams. While his wages were not especially high, his coworkers were friendly and the environment was positive, so that the probation officer encouraged him to keep working there without looking for a different job. His exam preparations, undertaken while he was working and studying, led to success in the entrance exam for a night high school; since then his life has remained stable and his probation has officially concluded.

With regard to case study 1, the Report states that the youth's delinquency arose from rapidly falling in with bad company while his parents, working nights, were unable to supervise him, with the repeated delinquency after parole occurring along exactly the same lines. In general, youths with friends who commit delinquency find rehabilitation opportunities in their parents' suitable supervision, employment or schooling, or in some cases a change of environment due to moving house.

The discussion of this case study indicates that because the youth's parents were focused on work and unable to supervise him, and because of the lack of social resources in the region that he could call on as a foreigner, methods and approaches to preventing his recidivism were limited.

With regard to case study 2, the Report's discussion concludes that factors in stabilizing the youth's life included his mother's decision to move house when preparing living arrangements for him out of concern about his friendships, his ability to continue working after parole with the encouragement of his probation officer, and the fact that, when he proposed to enter high school, the availability of social resources such as a tutoring school for young foreigners along with his own efforts made it possible for him to do so. In addition, it notes that the points he himself raises—that while he had been bullied in school, everyone at the detention center treated him fairly in the same way as the Japanese youths, and that he was able to continue work because his colleagues accepted him and never made fun of him—constitute reference information when considering the treatment of foreign young people who have committed delinquency.

The senior coordinator of a juvenile detention center told me that whether parolees turn to rehabilitation or to recidivism is determined by the following two points: whether they are able to attain a stable lifestyle (schooling, employment, a place to feel at home) and whether they are able to cut contact with friends who engage in delinquency. The case studies above suggest a similar argument. Let us look at T's case once again. T entered juvenile detention in October 2003, received his junior high school diploma there in March 2004, and left on parole in November 2004. He was taken in by his parents at their home. A probation officer visited the house regularly and encouraged him to be careful about negative friendships, but when the bad crowd that he used to spend time with saw him on the street, they began to invite him out repeatedly. He left his bakery job after a week due to staying out too late at night. Looking back on that time, T's mother recalls that his bad Japanese friends' insistence that he join them seemed like a nightmare, and that she had been too busy at work to take good care of T.

The Report notes that in comparison with Japanese delinquent young people, one disadvantage in growth that foreign delinquent young people are likely to face relates to their parents' capacity to supervise. Although the role played by parents in cutting off negative friendships is significant, in many cases the parents' supervisory capacity is deeply insufficient. In addition to the problem of being too taken up with work to look after their children sufficiently, parents' limited Japanese ability makes communication with probation officers difficult and negatively affects recidivism. Even after spending twenty years in Japan, T's mother's Japanese skills are limited to simple greetings.

The senior coordinator mentioned above says that he sometimes feels qualms about entrusting his parolees to their parents. However, if the parents volunteer to take their children in, he cannot enforce other options. Another supervising coordinator says that for all intents and purposes, parents are the only ones taking in young people who have just finished compulsory education.

Perhaps there was some laxity in T's parents' supervision. However, it is also true that they faced multiple conditions making supervision difficult: needing to work at night, limited Japanese ability making communication problematic, and so on. As a result, T found himself in an environment where cutting off negative friendships was difficult when he returned to his parents' house and their limited capacity to supervise.

Case study 2 shows that factors playing a major role in stabilizing that young person's life included his mother's decision to move house out of concern about his negative friendships, the probation officer's well-placed encouragement which helped him stay employed, and the environment which enabled him to make use of social resources such as a tutoring school. T's mother describes her "nightmare" with misery. "It really was his bad Japanese friends from junior high school who destroyed our lives. We always taught T right from wrong. But those bad junior high school friends were the worst luck he ever had, and the beginning of the destruction of our lives." (T's mother)

The Report argues that while there are no major differences in the elements required for treatment of foreign delinquent youth and of their Japanese counterparts (suitable education, stable employment, improved household environments, no contact with delinquent friends), the former are more likely to find the process of achieving these difficult, and that special measures are required to overcome these difficulties (p.79).

Going to High School Was Never Considered

T, who had been unable to find a place to learn in junior high school, treasured the one he found during juvenile detention. The Report above notes that almost all 90 detainees of foreign nationality were able to improve their Japanese ability or maintain a level of everyday conversation or above while in detention. T likewise looks back with pleasure on the painstaking Japanese education he received there. About three months after his parole, T began to look for part-time work through the HelloWork labor exchange; was this really his only option, as opposed to enrolling in high school?

It is possible to take high school entrance exams or find employment while in juvenile detention. In T's case, as he had been detained on a year's basis and received his junior high school diploma in March, about six months in, taking the exams would have been nearly impossible at the point of junior high school graduation. Paroled in 2005, it would have been in the spring of 2006 that he took the exams. "I couldn't imagine going to high school because I couldn't do the work in junior high," he said, but in fact about 30% of students at part-time high schools have a background of school non-attendance.

While the data is somewhat out of date, a look at the

status and characteristics of part-time and correspondence high school students shows that of the former, 31.3% have a background of school non-attendance and 3.0% are of foreign nationality, while for the latter the figures are 14.6% and 0.6% respectively (from the 2011 MEXT-commissioned project "Survey Research on Part-Time and Correspondence High School Curricula," National Part-Time/Correspondence High School Education Promotion Association). The numbers of high school students requiring Japanese language instruction in FY 2008 were highest at day schools, but in FY 2010 part-time high schools surpassed day schools and have continued to increase in comparison. The most recent figures (FY 2014) show a total of 2,915 students, including 1,547 part-time students (53.1%), 1,351 day students (46.3%), and 17 correspondence students (0.5%). More than half the students requiring Japanese language instruction are enrolled in part-time high schools.

Factors encouraging foreign students to enroll in part-time and correspondence high schools include, first, the low barrier to matriculation, which is considerably easier in terms of the academic ability required at part-time high schools than day high schools. Correspondence high schools essentially enroll all comers, on the basis of "any time, anyone, anywhere." Second, a major component is that part-time and correspondence high schools' student bodies are highly diverse in age, nationality, and background, with school cultures and environments that make learning easier, unlike the academic ability-oriented, group-based, uniform atmosphere of day high schools. Part-time and correspondence curricula are promising educational paths for students with experience of non-attendance or those requiring Japanese language support.

In the present era in which 99% of Japanese students enroll in high school, in order to settle into Japanese society for the long term, high school enrollment is one of the minimum conditions for career formation among foreign students as well. In addition, the goal of high school enrollment can be a major motivating force for rehabilitation.

One of the reasons that high school enrollment never occurred to T as an option was his disconnection from junior high school. Various reasons come to mind—he had attended for only a few months, the school was not informed that he was in juvenile detention, the detention center was far away—but in any case, no one from his junior high school ever came to visit while he was in detention. His "graduation" occurred around the midpoint of his time in detention, but apparently no one raised the possibility of high school enrollment there either. Elsewhere, his parents recall that they had never heard of part-time high schools. No one around T was able to provide him with information or support for high school enrollment.

Upon attending a presentation on life experiences at a part-time high school in north Kanto, I noted that all 15 presenters had experience of school non-attendance. Almost all of them talked about how hard it had been, before describing the various ways they had discovered the part-time curriculum and the pleasure of being able to learn. Part-time high schools are home to many students with backgrounds of non-attendance and foreign students needing Japanese language support. It is impossible not to think that, with someone to provide him with sufficient information and support, T too might have been able to enter a part-time high school.

The Balance of Crime and Punishment

T's application for renewal of his status of residence was rejected while he was in prison, making him an illegal overstayer; the very day he was granted provisional release, deportation proceedings against him began and he was detained in an immigration control facility. The Immigration Control Act regulates, while maintaining that deportation and criminal proceedings are separate, that in general deportation proceedings are to be executed after criminal proceedings are complete.

These legal proceedings mean that there is no opportunity to realize the outcomes of the corrective education or rehabilitative projects taken on in juvenile detention or prison with an eye to parole, provisional release, or completion of the sentence served. When detained in an immigration facility immediately upon one of these measures, surely anyone would fall into despair. The director of a juvenile detention center, who has seen youths taken away by immigration agents on the day of their parole many times, says that he has wept over those who had made their best efforts while in detention.

Another detention center director and a senior coordinator also used words like “frustrating”, “painful,” and so on.

Cases like this have been considered problematic based on concepts such as the balance of crime and punishment, and double jeopardy. On this point, let us refer first to Kiyoto Tanno’s discussion of the problem of deportation proceedings executed against foreign young people who have committed delinquency (Tanno, 2017).

Young person B came to Japan from Peru at age 10 in 1992, summoned by his mother, who had gone to Japan to work. Unable to adapt to school life in sixth grade, at the end of his first year in junior high school he fell into bad company whom he felt comfortable with. While he spent more of his time with them, school was the only place he had to go, and he continued to attend and, on a teacher’s recommendation, entered a part-time high school. However, he was unable to follow the classes, and dropped out two months in, after a violent incident. Although he found a job, he still went along with his friends, participating in theft and sniffing paint thinner without seeing the severity of these actions, and ending up in juvenile detention. After leaving the detention center, he was sentenced to eighteen months in prison for the theft of a washing machine, with a five-year suspended sentence (on probation). A year after the verdict, his grandmother—the only person he was close to—passed away, and he became emotionally unstable, falling into bad company again and receiving a three-year prison sentence for violations of the Stimulants Control

Act and Road Traffic Act. His mother's application to renew his status of residence was rejected while he was in prison, making him an illegal overstayer, and deportation proceedings were brought immediately.

B's legal defense focused most strongly on the perspective of the balance of crime and punishment. "What must be considered is that after receiving a sentence involving the severe disadvantages of physical restraint and forcible movement (note: in B's case, three years' imprisonment), deportation proceedings take place for the exact same social reasons" (p.76). The defense argued that while in formal terms deportation may be an administrative penalty, when evaluated as effectively a concurrent sentence, it should be considered double jeopardy; in particular, for foreigners who came to Japan in early childhood, grew up there, and have built a life in Japan, deportation proceedings are tantamount to losing their entire basis of living and should be considered a concurrent sentence. They added that based on this stance, B's delinquency and crimes should not be considered his responsibility alone, that his long stay in Japan had essentially eradicated his basis of living in his country of origin and that forcible deportation would thus put his human dignity at risk and leave his family scattered.

B's case is clearly similar to T's in many ways. Both came to Japan at age ten with families of Japanese heritage; both found places to be in junior high school with bad company; both (in junior high school for T and high school for B) were sentenced to juvenile detention for theft and other delinquent acts. Both were sentenced to prison for crimes committed after leaving detention, and lost their status of residence while in prison. B lodged an objection to his deportation order in mid-2007 at age 25, when he had been in Japan for 15 years. The major differences between B and T are the makeup of their families and their roles therein. The defense argued that B's family (his mother, for whom illness made long hours of work difficult, and his younger sister) depended on his salary, and that he was a father-figure for his sister.

About a year after this incident, B received special permission to remain and was granted long-term resident status (his mother and sister are permanent residents). Tanno points out that a major factor in the immigration authorities' decision to grant special permission to remain may have been, rather than the rationale involved, the overwhelming amount of material on the family's life, showing their relations and basis of living (p.83).

Let us consider T's case once again from the perspective of the balance of crime and punishment. T was arrested on charges of robbery and sentenced to seven years' imprisonment. In prison, his father's application on his behalf for renewal of his status of residence was rejected, and he became an illegal overstayer. Unquestionably, the seven years' imprisonment played a major role in this decision on the part of Immigration Control. T remained in prison as an illegal overstayer for several years and was granted provisional release, on the very day of which he was detained in an immigration facility. He has remained there for over two years.

The issue of the concurrent sentence is that the administrative penalty of deportation causes as much or more pain as the actual prison sentence, and that the degree of this pain is determined largely by the state of the subject's life in Japan. The key here is the two items also confirmed in B's case: family relations and the basis of living.

"Seven years is a heavy sentence. Twenty years is a long time." This is what one lawyer said when asked for an opinion on T's case. A legal examination of the suitability of T's seven-year sentence in response to his crime cannot be done here, but his seven-year sentence became the basis for the rejection of his status of residence renewal application and the absolute evidence confirming his malice. In addition, his work toward rehabilitation in prison was excluded from evaluation, with no effect on the confirmation of his malice at all.

The influence of deportation on its subject is completely different for a temporary resident with no real basis of living in Japan and for one whose basis of living is restricted to Japan alone. The greatest pain is inflicted by deportation on foreigners for whom it means being cut off from family and returned to their countries of origin with no basis for living.

There is no question of T's family returning to Brazil, given the following circumstances as well. "If T has to go back, we might be able to send him a little money, but that's it. Our priority is taking care of our younger son. He tried and failed to adapt to Brazil, so we're living in Japan as a family. It's going to be hard for T to manage in Brazil after twenty years, so if possible we'd like to live together in Japan" (T's mother). T's mother also says that they are no longer in touch with relatives in Brazil. "Our relatives in Japan (my husband's nephew and so on) criticize us now because T committed a crime. They've told all our relatives about it since going back to Brazil. The family in Brazil has told us not to rely on them or look for them. They've cut off contact already" (T's mother).

"I thought about going back to Brazil at one point to take care of my brother when he was sick, and our family returned there in the summer of 2012, but my younger son, who was born in Japan, couldn't handle it and we decided to live in Japan" (T's father's, Inquiry Record, March 31, 2015, p.6).

For T, deportation from Japan would mean being torn from his family and deprived of the entire basis of living developed since early childhood, exposing him to great pain. Likewise, his deportation would obviously cause his family to suffer great pain and damage as well. He says that "because we were in Japan, I couldn't attend the deathbeds of my grandpa and grandma whom I loved a lot. If they send me back to Brazil, I won't be able to see the deathbeds of my parents." For Japanese, the opportunity to return to society is granted after the fulfillment of criminal responsibility. For T, even after having fulfilled his responsibility with seven years in prison, this fact itself has driven him into a situation even more painful than imprisonment. The perspective of the balance of crime and punishment finds that, in comparison with his crime, the punishment imposed on him is all too severe.

Long-term detention in an immigration facility is likewise problematic from the same perspective. Provisional release is denied, repeatedly, for undisclosed reasons. There is no way to know when it will be possible to leave the facility. It may not even be possible to see family. There is no way to know when deportation proceedings will take place. Beset by unease of this kind, each day is spent in an environment riddled with contamination. Long-term detention, completely subject to the whims of immigration control, can often be more painful for the detainees than a limited-term prison sentence.

Three Dreams

"Right now, my first dream is still to get out of the Immigration Agency Higashi-Nihon Immigration Center. Provisional release is a wish in my imagination. But the dream I hope comes true in the near future is, even if I get provisional release, first I want to thank God and pray and praise him. I'd like to go back to the apartment and spend time with my parents and talk. I want to be a good son to make my second dream come true. My third dream is to be with my brother and take care of him too. Finally, my last dream is to go back to school so I can start my life over. If I can be useful to Japanese society, I want to do that. Please let me be useful. I think that I should be useful. I'm going to pray to God to let me learn and let the Japanese government respond to my positive interest in learning right now. There might not be a way in XX Prefecture for me to go back to school in Japan. But I want to go to a night junior high school, I don't have the academic background I need so I want to go to a night junior high school myself. I'm not going to change my mind. I like studying. If it goes well, another dream is to go to high school and then go to college and study theology." (letter, partially corrected)

Conclusion

T's twenty years in Japan can be summed up as a continual vicious circle. Coming to Japan at the behest of others, changing elementary schools and being unable to enter junior high school with friends, the lack of special Japanese instruction in junior high school, falling into non-attendance soon after enrollment due to bullying and difficulty with studying, finding himself at home with a delinquent group rather than at school or in his own home, being unable to cut contact with them and committing delinquency again after parole from juvenile detention, the lack of anyone to offer advice or support for high school enrollment, suddenly losing the job he had found on his second parole, meeting C (who later induced him to robbery) while working in a factory, becoming an illegal overstayer while in prison, being unable to return to society after parole from prison, having his applications for provisional release all rejected during the crackdown on overstayers, and being deported to his country of origin after three years of detention. This vicious circle is closely related to the absence of educational policy for foreign children, and to that of anyone who could have supported T's schoolwork and high school enrollment.

Looking at T's case from the perspective of the balance between crime and punishment, his punishment has far exceeded the severity of his crime: the administrative penalty of deportation has conferred on him as much or more pain than the actual prison sentence. One major punishment was his three years in detention at the immigration facility. During this time, his applications for provisional release were all rejected, so that his longing to see his family was never fulfilled. There is no doubt that long-term detention with no end in sight is more painful for the detainees than a limited-term prison sentence. The other major punishment was his forcible deportation to his country of origin. The pain of deportation is completely different for a temporary resident with no stable basis of living in Japan and for one whose basis of living is restricted to Japan alone. T and his family lived in Japan for twenty years, losing their basis of living in Brazil, the country to which T was compelled to return, an action which tore him away from his family.

T's punishment is deeply interconnected with the absolute authority of the immigration authorities. Takaya (2017) points out that the legal system permitting a wide range of discretion to the immigration authorities on the expulsion of illegal overstayers and the determination of special permission to remain was constructed during the postwar occupation and has been maintained along the same lines ever since. The justicial decisions concerning sentencing to juvenile detention or to prison consider the weight of individual delinquency or crimes and determine the type of juvenile detention center and the length of the detainment or imprisonment period. In contrast, the immigration authorities consider all illegal overstayers to be uniformly malicious, with no consideration for individual circumstances, and have absolute authority over the issuance of deportation orders and over judgments on special permission to remain and the validity of provisional release applications. Justicial decisions are not involved with these administrative measures. Further, because of this wide range of discretion, trials almost never find that the immigration authorities have exceeded or abused their authority.

This book has examined the many complex factors which led T to delinquency and crime, all of which have been absolutely ignored by the immigration authorities and the courts. The immigration authorities argued that, regardless of reason or purpose, illegal overstay is malicious. The courts dismissed every effort made to atone for crimes and return, rehabilitated, to society as of no influence on this malice. The responsibility for crimes committed within a complex context was placed entirely on the individual alone, with all efforts toward redress, including atonement, wholly dismissed.

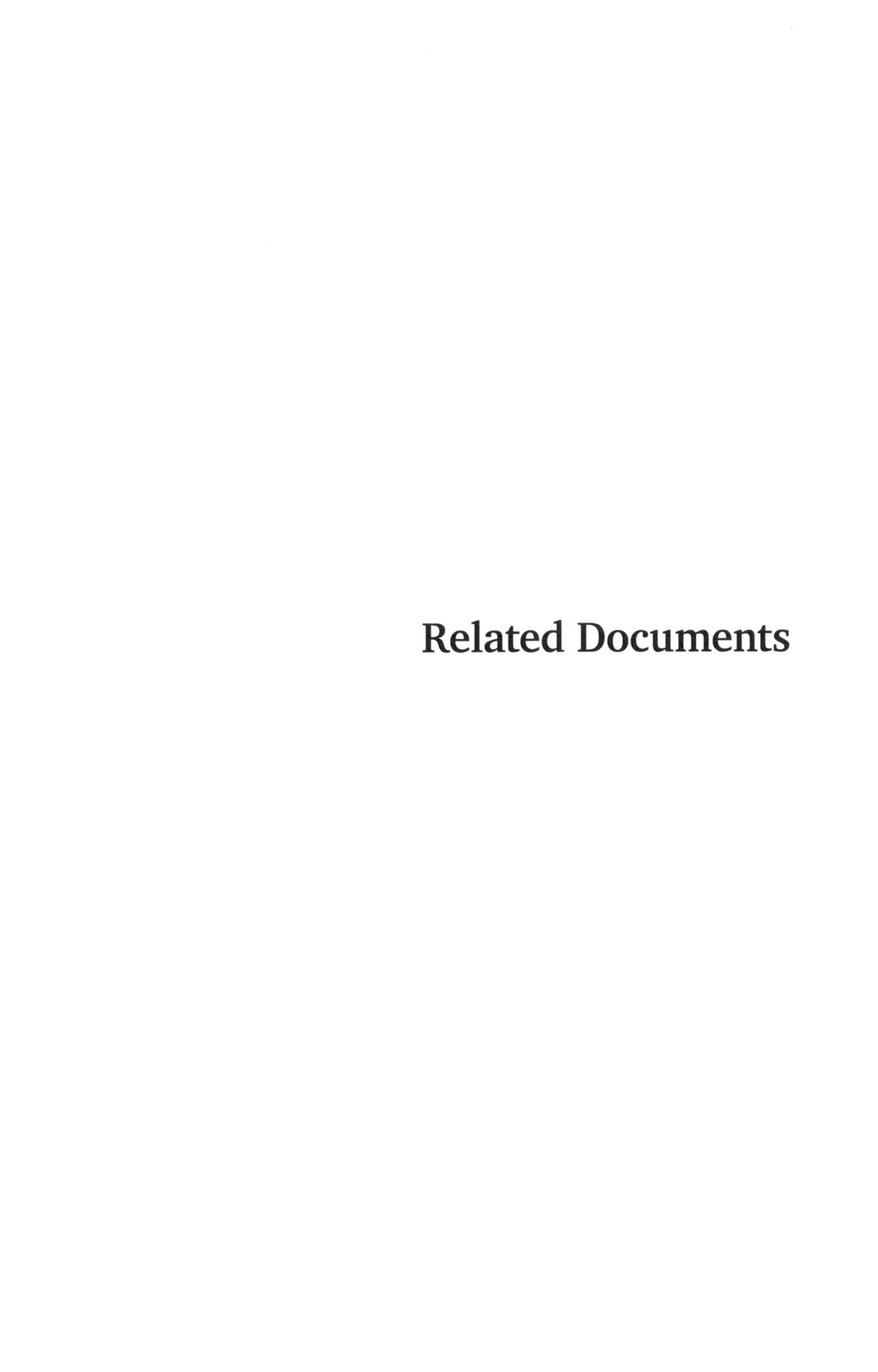

Related Documents

Related Documents 1

Statement

To the Tokyo District Court

October 4, 2017

My family is in Japan. My family will go on living in Japan. I don't have family in Brazil. I want to live with my family. Also, I have been in Japan for nineteen years, since I was a child. I left Brazil and came to Japan in 1998 when I was only ten years old. My brother has been born and raised in Japan.

I have lived in Japan for a long time and can no longer speak Portuguese well. I have spent about two-thirds of my life in Japan. I don't know anyone in Brazil and I can't speak the language. So it would be very difficult for me to live in Brazil. For these reasons, I want to live in Japan and I don't think I can live anywhere else.

It's true that I have committed crimes in the past. I admitted to them, took my punishment, and atoned for my crimes. In the past, I couldn't speak either Japanese or Portuguese well and I couldn't fit in with the people around me, so I ended up falling into bad company. I wanted to apologize to the victim of the robbery that I was sent to prison for, and to compensate them, but I haven't ever been able to leave since being arrested, and I don't have any money, so I still can't apologize or give them compensation. But if I get to leave in the future, I still want to do that.

Also, of course, I will never commit another crime. In prison I worked hard and also studied hard. I used a sewing machine to make purses and athletic supporters, and also a product called SecureFit that keeps seatbelts from digging into babies in car child seats. I also used a sander on wooden and metal parts and worked with drivers and tackers. I worked on making parts for chairs, doors, faucets, the bullet train, and so on.

I was punished six times in prison, but three of them weren't because I did anything bad, it was that I wasn't getting along with my cellmates and wanted to change cells, and the officer in charge said I had to go to the punishment block to get my room changed, so that's what I did. Also, I got punished for unauthorized laundry, because I washed towels even though the prison rule was that you couldn't wash towels with soap. There was a fight too, because the other guy hit me, so I had to fight back to defend myself. None of them were serious punishments, and I had fewer than most of the inmates. Also, until entering prison I always renewed my status of residence and the applications were always accepted. Even after I went to prison, my family applied for renewal for me, but the application was rejected. That's why I became an overstayer.

Until I was arrested for my crime, I experienced various kinds of work. I had a forklift license and a crane operator's qualifications. Now my Japanese is better, and if I am allowed to stay in Japan, I can earn my living here and support my family. I am finally old enough to work for my parents and do my duty as a good son. I want to stay in Japan for my family's sake. And I want to be useful to Japanese society.

My parents want to live in Japan with me. I also want to live in Japan where my family is. My parents and my brother have a life in Japan and can't make a different one in Brazil. So if I go to Brazil, our family will be separated. And as long as I can't come back to Japan, we will never be able to live together again. My family cannot travel frequently back and forth between Brazil and Japan. I may have relatives in Brazil, but I have never seen or contacted them since coming to Japan, so I don't even know where they are.

My Japanese is better than my Portuguese now. I understand simple Portuguese, but nothing else. My father is an educated man and I don't always understand his Portuguese. There are a lot of Brazilians at the Higashi-Nihon Immigration Center where I am being detained now, but I can't communicate with them.

My parents and my brother will always be my parents and my brother. It would be unbearably painful never to be able to see my family again. I understand that I am being deported because I broke the law, but I hope that you will consider once again how terrible this pain is and give me a chance to remain in Japan and make up for what I have done. When I was young, I didn't listen to my parents and caused a lot of trouble. But I have seen the error of my ways, worked hard, and grown up. I am not the same as I was. From now on, for my family's sake, I want to obey the laws and rules and do my best in Japan.

Related Documents 2

To the Minister of Justice and the Director of the Higashi-Nihon Immigration Center

April 12, 2019

Petition

My name is Matsuo Tamaki, a faculty member at Utsunomiya University. I submit this petition in the hope of receiving your particular consideration for the application for provisional release placed by T, currently detained at the Higashi-Nihon Immigration Center.

I came to know T last May through his use of the Japanese-Portuguese study dictionary of which I was editor-in-chief. Thereafter I have visited him on average at least once a month, discussing various matters. I have read the full record of the administrative litigation he lodged with the Tokyo District Court and Tokyo High Court.

I have spent over a decade researching the issue of education for foreign children in Japan, as well as engaging in practical activities that contribute to local communities. While it is a fact that children who come to Japan at school age without much Japanese ability often become isolated, stop attending school, and take up antisocial activities, I have also seen children who, granted sufficient opportunity to learn through understanding and cooperation from those around them, develop into individuals who are able to contribute greatly to Japanese society.

T, who came to Japan at age ten without a word of Japanese, stopped attending junior high school shortly after enrollment due to bullying and difficulty with academics, changed jobs frequently after his graduation, committed a crime and served his time in prison for it, lost his status of residence in prison, and became an "illegal overstayer." The pattern of his downfall is unique to foreign children in Japan. It is unfortunate that his surroundings were not able to offer him support when he stopped attending school.

At this time, he deeply regrets his past errors and hopes strongly to "go back to school," "try again," "be a good son," "look after [his] younger brother," and "contribute to Japanese society" in Japan. I have sensed his heartfelt longing to these ends every time I visit him. I cannot but hope that Japanese society, with its aims of becoming a truly multicultural society, will look favorably on T's longing to "go back to school" and "try again." I ask once again that particular consideration be given to T's application for provisional release.

Matsuo Tamaki
Professor, School of International Studies, Utsunomiya University

Related Documents 3

Justices' Constitutional Interpretation of "Long-Term Detention" in Taiwan and Amendments to Immigration Law

I.Interpretations of the Constitutional Court, Judicial Yuan, No.708 [The Immigration Detention of Foreign Nationals Pending Deportation Case] February 6, 2013

Source: Constitutional Court, Judicial Yuan
https://cons.judicial.gov.tw/jcc/en-us/jep03/show?expno=708

◎ Issue

Is it constitutional to not provide prompt judicial remedy to a foreign national who is facing deportation and being temporarily detained by the National Immigration Agency? Is it constitutional to not have a court review of an extension of a foreign national's temporary detention?

◎ Reasoning

Article 38, Paragraph 1 of the Act (as amended on December 26, 2007) provides: "[t]he National Immigration Agency may temporarily detain a foreign national under any of the following circumstances ..." (this is the same as the provision promulgated on November 23, 2011: "[t]he National Immigration Agency may temporarily detain a foreign national under any of the following circumstances ...") (hereinafter the “disputed provision”). ... It is not unconstitutional that the disputed provision allows a temporary detention for a reasonable period due to the repatriation operation. ... Nevertheless, the disputed provision can hardly be deemed to have sufficiently protected the fundamental human rights of detainees, because it does not afford temporary detainees with prompt and effective judicial remedies. Therefore, the disputed provision violates due process of law under Article 8, Paragraph 1 of the Constitution. Furthermore, the disputed provision’s allowance for the Agency to extend the temporary detention without court review also contravenes the aforementioned meaning and purpose of personal freedom protection under the Constitution. ...The unconstitutional portions of the disputed provision shall become null and void if they have not been amended within two years from the issuance of this Interpretation.

II.Immigration Act

Source: Laws & Regulations Database of The Republic of China
https://law.moj.gov.tw/ENG/LawClass/LawAll.aspx?pcode=D0080132

Amended November 16, 2016

Chapter 6 Deportation and Detention (Articles 36 to 39)

Article 38 (partial translation)

An alien who is sentenced to forcible deportation and falls under any of the following circumstances may be temporarily detained by the National Immigration Agency if a compulsory exit order is difficult or impractical to enforce. The duration of temporary detention may not exceed 15 days. The alien shall be allowed to submit claims before the temporary detention order is implemented.

Article 38-4 (full translation)

Prior to the deadline of the temporary detention and whether it is necessary to continue the detention sanction, the National Immigration Agency shall apply for a continuation of the detention period by submitting the reasons to the court no later than 5 days before the deadline.

In case the detainee's passport or travel document is lost or expired with no replacement, or reissued or extended prior to the deadline of the continued detention and whenever it is necessary to continue the detention sanction, the National Immigration Agency shall apply for an extension of the detention period by submitting the reasons to the court no later than 5 days before the deadline.

The period of continued detention shall not exceed forty-five (45) days from the deadline of temporary detention; the period of extended detention shall not exceed forty (40) days from the deadline of continued detention.

References

Books

- Immigration Problems Research Association. (2001). *Nyukan shuyo shisetsu: Sweden, Austria, Rengo okoku, soshite Nihon (Immigration detention facilities in Sweden, Austria, the United Kingdom, and Japan)* Gendaijinbunsha.
- Kodama, Koichi. (2010). “Zairyu tokubetsu kyoka wo meguru saibanrei no keiko (Trends in court cases on special permission to remain)” in Atsushi Kondo, Yoshikazu Shiobara, Eriko Suzuki eds. *Hiseiki taizaisha to zairyu tokubetsu kyoka: Ijusha no kako/genzai/mirai (Unofficial residents and special permission to remain: The past, present, and future of migrants)*, Nippon Hyoronsha, pp.131-41.
- Minamikawa, Fuminori.(2016). “Shinjiyushugi jidai no kokusai imin to kokkyo kanri: Kokkyo kiki ni taiji shite (International migration and border control in the neoliberalist era: Facing a border crisis),” in Kiyoshi Matsushita and Ken Fujita eds., *Global South to wa nani ka (What is the Global South?)*, Minerva Shobo, pp. 145-164.
- Nakajima, Shin’ichiro. (2010). “Nyukan gyosei no ‘akazu no mon’ e no chosen: Taikyo kyosei meireisho happu shobun go no zairyu tokubetsu kyoka wo shutoku shita yottsu no kazoku no jirei (Taking on the immigration authorities’ ‘closed door’: Four case studies of families who obtained special permission to stay after being served with deportation orders),” in Atsushi Kondo, Yoshikazu Shiobara, Eriko

Suzuki eds., *Hiseiki taizaisha to zairyu tokubetsu kyoka: Ijusha tachi no kako/genzai/mirai (Unofficial residents and special permission to remain: The past, present, and future of migrants)* pp. 145-164.

- Sakanaka, Hidenori, and Toshio Saito. (2012). *Shutsunyukoku kanri oyobi nanmin nintei ho: Chikujo kaisetsu [Kaitei dai-yon-ban] (An article-by-article interpretation of the Immigration Control and Refugee Recognition Act [4th revision])*, Nihon Kajo Shuppan.
- Takaya, Sachi. (2017). *Tsuiho to teiko no politics (The politics of expulsion and resistance)*, Nakanishiya Shuppan.
- Takaya, Sachi ed. (2019). *Imin seisaku to wa nani ka: Nihon no genjitsu kara kangaeru (Considering immigration policy from the status quo in Japan)*, Jimbun Shoin.
- Tamaki, Matsuo. (2017). *Mirai wo hiraku anata e: "Tomo ni ikiru" shakai wo kangaeru tame no 10 sho (To you, the future pioneer: Ten chapters for thinking about a "coexistent" society)*, Shimotsuke Shimbunsha.
- Tamaki, Matsuo. (2018). "Gaikokujin seito no manabi no ba to shinro hosho: Tabunka kyosei wo ninau jisedai shien (Learning spaces and guaranteed future paths for foreign children: Supporting the next generation responsible for the multicultural society"), in School of International Studies, Utsunomiya University ed. *Tabunka kyosei wo do toraeru ka (Approaches to multiculturalism)*, Shimotsuke Shimbunsha.
- Tanno, Kiyoto. (2018). *Gaikokujin no jinken no shakaigaku (The sociology of "foreigner's rights")*, Yoshida Shoten.

- Tokyo Metropolitan Research Group on Advice for Foreigners. (2013). *Kaitei gaikokujin yorozu sodan: Jirei to kaito 120 (Revised all-purpose advice for foreigners: 120 case studies and responses)*, Nihon Kajo Shuppan.
- Yabe, Takeshi. (2009). *Shonen'in wo deta ato de: Kosei dekiru hito, dekinai hito (After leaving juvenile detention: Those who can and cannot achieve rehabilitation)* Gendaijinbunsha.
- Yamada, Ryoichi, and Tadamasa Kuroki. (2010). *Yoku wakaru nyukan ho: Dai-ni-ban (The Immigration Control Act made easy: 2nd edition)* Yuhikaku.

Papers

- Go, Taesung. (2017). "Shuyo to karihomen ga utsushidasu nyukan seisaku mondai: Ushiku Shuyosho wo jirei ni (Immigration policy problems seen through detention and provisional release: The case of the Ushiku Detention Center)" in *Osaka Keizai Hoka Daigaku Asia Taiheiyo Kenkyusho Center Nenpo (Center for Asia Pacific Partnership Report)* (14), pp.32-39.
- Go, Taesung. (2019). "Nikkan ni okeru gaikokujin shuyo shisetsu no hikaku kento: Choki shuyo mondai wo chushin ni (Comparative examination of detention facilities for foreigners in Japan and South Korea: Focusing on the problem of long-term detention)" in *Asia Taiheiyo Kenkyusho Center Nenpo (Center for Asia Pacific Partnership Report)* (16) pp.17-25.
- Higuchi, Naoto, and Nanako Inaba. (2018). "Kangeki wo

nuu: Newcomer dai-ni-sedai no daigaku shingaku (Threading through the gaps: University enrollment among second-generation newcomers)" in *Shakaigaku hyoron (Japanese Sociological Review)* 58, pp.567-583.

- Takaya, Sachi. (2018). "Gaikokujin rodosha kara 'fuho taizaisha' e: 1980-nendai iko no Nihon ni okeru hiseiki taizaisha wo meguru category no hensen to kiketsu (From foreign workers to 'illegal overstayers': Shifts and consequences in categories of unofficial residents in Japan from the 1980s on)" in *Shakaigaku hyoron (Japanese Sociological Review)* 68, pp.531-548.
- Tanno, Kiyoto. (2007). "Zairyu tokubetsu kyoka no shakaigaku: Nihon de kurasu gaikokujin no hoteki kiso (The sociology of special permission to stay: The legal basis for foreigners living in Japan)" in *Ohara Shakai Mondai Kenkyusho Zasshi (Journal of Ohara Institute for Social Research)* No. 582, pp.1-30.

Others

- Immigration Control Bureau, Ministry of Justice (November 2017). *Taikyo Kyousei Gyomu Ni Tsuite.(Deportation Duties)*.
- Immigration Control Bureau, Ministry of Justice (December 2018). *Taikyo Kyousei Gyomu Ni Tsuite.(Deportation Duties)*.
- Majima, Madoka. (2007). *Teiju gaikokujin kyosei sokan ni tsuite no ho shakaigakuteki kenkyu: Nihon ni okeru dainisedai ni kansuru jirei wo chushin ni shite (Legal-sociological research on the forcible deportation of long-term resident*

foreigners: Focusing on cases among the second generation in Japan). Master's thesis for thof Social Sciences, Hitotsubashi University.

- MOJ Research and Training Institute Report 51. (2013). *Rainichi gaikokujin syounen no hikou ni kansuru kenkyuu(Research on Delinquency Among Foreign Youths in Japan)* (Report No. XX).
- National Part-Time/Correspondence High School Education Promotion Association. (2012). *Koutougakkou teijisei katei, tsuushinsei katei no arikata ni kansuru chousakenkyuu(Survey Research on Part-Time and Correspondence High School Curricula)* (2009-2011 MEXT-commissioned project).
- Japan Association for Refugees (October 13, 2016). "Questions for the Higashi-Nihon Immigration Center" , from https://www.refugee.or.jp/jar/report/2016/10/13-0000.shtml (last accessed August 3, 2018).
- Provisional Release Association in Japan (PRAJ) (June 2018). "What is Immigration Control's Purpose in Long-Term Detention?", from http://praj-praj.blogspot.com/2018/06/blog-post_27.html (last accessed July 28, 2019).
- White Paper on Crime. (2018). Aging and Crimes (ed. Ministry of Justice Research and Training Institute).

Trial Records

- Appeal, August 31, 2016, April 24, 2017.
- Evidence Statements, May 12, July 6, September 7, 2017, April 2, 2018.

- First Prepared Document, August 30, 2017.
- Inquiry Record, June 1, 2010, March 31, 2015, August 10, 2016.
- Opening Statement, October 14, 2010.
- Oral Inquiry Record, August 31, 2016.
- Responses, July 6, 2017, May 10, 2018.
- Statements, November 11, 2010, October 4, 2017.
- Statement Records, June 1, 2010, February 3, 2015, March 31, 2015.
- Suit, April 24, 2017.
- Verdicts, December 16, 2010, January 25, 2018, June 28, 2018.

Afterword

The information and data used here were mainly collected through the following methods. (1) Visits with T: 16 visits to T in detention, from May 2018 through November 2019. (2) Exchange of letters: T responded to various questions and described his life in detention upon request, in twenty-odd letters and postcards. (3) Reading of the entire administrative litigation trial records and part of the criminal trial records, provided by the lawyers in charge. (4) Interviews with the lawyers in charge: three interviews with the administrative litigation lawyer and one with the criminal lawyer. (5) Interviews with T's mother: three interviews, one in his father's presence as well, although it was his mother who responded to almost all the questions). (6) Interview with a staff member from the Regional Parole Board. (7) Visits to juvenile detention centers: three centers visited (including the two where T was detained).

I asked T to read the manuscript which has become this book; his reaction to the draft was "It's well written." I have no way of knowing what feelings this brief reaction was intended to convey. He also thanked me for making it widely known in his stead that people like him exist. However, I was honestly nervous about how he would react to the manuscript. Much of its contents touched on bad memories for him, and yet I had gone ahead and asked him to recall them over and over. Faced with his twenty years reconfigured in writing, perhaps he was drawn back to the inexpressible events he had faced during that time, as well as finding it painfully evocative of despair and regret. In a sense, this book has been a process of excavating T's twenty years together.

In May and June 2018, I took some students to do fieldwork. We visited T's home twice, first with three students, then with two. Both times, a student who could speak Portuguese served as T's mother's interpreter. Two students accompanied me to the first juvenile detention center, and one to the interview with the former Regional Parole Board member. One student attended the presentation on July 12 by a former Immigration Control staff member.

I also met with various people from May through July 2018. The lawyer Gen'ichi Yamaguchi and notary public Madoka Majima guided me through various case studies of deportation; it was Mr. Yamaguchi who had provided support when a family of acquaintances, former illegal overstayers (parents, daughter, and son) received special permission to remain. Their daughter put me in touch with Mr. Yamaguchi, enabling us to meet. Utsunomiya University Professor Emeritus Tadashi Imai provided opinions on T's case from the perspectives of international law and human rights; particularly notable points included that while appealing to international organizations on the grounds that long-term detention violated human rights would be possible, T was likely to be forcibly deported in that case, that T's failure to achieve rehabilitation after two periods of juvenile detention had probably influenced the verdict sentencing him to seven years' imprisonment, and that in reality trials go as the judge goes. I was also able to meet with Mr. Hosoda, the lawyer who handled T's criminal case, who referred to diaries of the time (almost a decade earlier) to answer my questions. In addition, while the District Prosecutor's Office refused me access to trial records on grounds of regulations, I was extremely fortunate to receive valuable documents from the time. I met several times with Kosuke Oie, the lawyer who handled T's administrative litigation, who provided a range of knowledge and information. Through the introduction of the Association Concerned with Issues at Ushiku Migrant Detention Center, I was able to exchange information and opinions with Taesung Go.

At three juvenile facilities, including the two where T was detained, I received painstaking explanations and facility tours from staff at the ranks of director, pastoral director, deputy director, senior coordinator, overall coordinator, and educational director. These visits originally came about when an acquaintance in Nagoya sent me a newspaper clipping about a juvenile detention center which had begun offering education in Portuguese, the native language of some detainees. This center, the first I visited, generously accepted my sudden request; then-Director Naoki Koshiba took it on himself to give me a thorough education since I had come so far, spending almost three hours with me. Around the same time, I was trying to visit T's juvenile detention centers and receiving little response; Director Koshiba's introduction helped open their doors for me. As well as realizing that juvenile detention centers are valuable places of learning for young people who have been involved in delinquency, I was able to get a real sense of T's experience. Director Koshiba, who also gave lectures at Utsunomiya University, has my sincere gratitude.

In late July 2018, I visited the Kaohsiung Detention Center and National Immigration Agency of Taiwan. While I had written a paper on "Status and Issues of Unofficially Resident Foreigners in Asia: Focusing on Japan, South Korea, and Taiwan" in 2008, I was still only minimally aware of the detention and deportation of illegal overstayers. Becoming aware of the long-term detention of illegal overstayers in Japan, I wanted to find out how matters stood in Taiwan and South Korea. I received three hours of time from the Observation and Deputy Chief at Kaohsiung Detention Center and two hours from a section head at the National Immigration Agency; at the former, I observed facility operation with consideration for detainees' human rights and safety. At the latter, I learned about the Agency's establishment in 2007 and its vision of multicultural respect and guaranteed migrant rights.

In response to the interpretation issued by the Taiwanese Constitutional Court of the Judicial Yuan in February 2013, the Immigration Act was amended in November 2016 to regulate that "detention of a person to be deported for over 15 days will require a court judgment" and "the time period of detention shall not exceed 100 days." I was told, on describing detention periods of over six months in Japan, that the same used to be the case in Taiwan, until the Immigration Act was amended in keeping with the Constitutional Court's interpretation that long-term detention violated the guarantee of the people's physical freedom. Japan has much to learn from Taiwan as it is now. My visit to Taiwan was made possible, with regard both to advance negotiation and to interpretation, by An-chun Cheng, Coordinator at the School of International Studies Center for the Multicultural Public Sphere.

I realize that much is left undone, and plan to consider future opportunities to address the issue of the authority given to Immigration Control in particular. There is no objective criterion for the judgment of whether to grant special permission to stay; it is made entirely based on this authority. The range of this authority granted to Immigration Control means that even if an appeal for the cancellation of a deportation order is lodged, the judgment made is that there was no significant excess or abuse of authority, and the plaintiff almost never wins their suit. At a gathering on July 12, a former Immigration Control staff member repeatedly used the phrase "Immigration Control mindset," saying that he had left the Bureau in part because of the system that allowed its judgments to sway the lives of individual humans and his fear of the administration which took no account of the many staff members troubled by this. This sense of "authority" or discretionary power may well be a key concept for the discussion of power structures in many fields of Japanese society.

Particularly helpful reference materials in the preparation of this book included Sachi Takaya's *The Politics of Expulsion and Resistance* (Nakanishiya Shuppan, 2017), Kiyoto Tanno's *The Sociology of "foreigner's rights"* (Yoshida Shoten, 2018), and Madoka Majima's "Legal-sociological research on the forcible deportation of long-term resident foreigners: Focusing on cases among the second generation in Japan" (master's thesis for the Graduate School of Social Sciences, Hitotsubashi University). Ms. Majima presented me with a copy of her thesis after my interview with Gen'ichi Yamaguchi. All have provided significant stimulation and helpful suggestions.

C, the ringleader of the robbery, was deported to Brazil several years ago. Before his deportation, he spoke with T's mother on the phone, apologizing for having gotten T involved in the robbery. C's mother sent T letters and gifts several times.

The Japanese government passed the revised Immigration Control Act in April 2019, revising their existing policy of "not recognizing foreign labor on principle in manual labor fields" to begin the full acceptance of foreign workers. It remains to be seen what form government's efforts will take to create a framework of acceptance for foreign workers and their children. As T did, many school-age children will come to Japan in the future, knowing no Japanese at all, full of mixed unease and expectation. How will Japanese society accept them, and what support will it offer?

す。しかし、イエスの役割というのは、その言葉に排他的な権威を持つ単なる道徳的立法者となることではありませんでした。イエスの到来の預言を遂行することがその役割であったのです。イエスには、神から与えられた使命と、その霊としての特別な性格による権威があったのです。イエスは、真なる命というものが地上においておこるものではなく、天の国において生きる命がそうであることを人類に教えに来たのです。この天の国へと導く道や、いかに神と調和するかの段を人々に教え、また人間の運命の実現のために訪れる事柄の流れの中に、その手段を感知することを人々に教えたのです。しかしながら、すべてを述べたのではなく、多くの点に関しては、イエス自身が述べたように、まだ理解されないであろう事柄について真実の種を蒔くにとどまったのでした。すべてについて触れながらも、言葉の裏に隠した形で伝えました。その言葉のいくつかに隠された意味が学び取られるには、新しい考えや新しい知識によって、それを理解するのに不可欠な鍵がもたらされることが必要でしたが、そうした考えというものは、人類の霊がある程度の水準に成熟しなければ顕すことができなかったのです。そうした考えを登場させ、発展させるために、科学は大いに貢献する必要がありました。したがって、科学が進歩するまで時間を与える必要があったのです。

His letter to the author, June 4, 2019

聖書にはあります。法務大臣は私達外国人を
さばいています。法務大臣の職員もその上の
おえらいさんも全員一人ずつさばかれます。
やつらは人間じゃない人間じゃない心がかり
人間はみないつかはかならず神にもさばかれ
れる日が来ます。私は反省してます。そして
神を一番に考えています。イエス・キリスト
が永遠の命なのです。せいれいは~~不思~~ふしぎ
なわざなどをするがるって一つと信じてます
。イエス・キリストを知って私は幸いです、

キリスト
イエスは法を破るために来たのではありませ
んが、その法とは神の法のことです。その法
を成就しに来た。つまり、その法を発展させ
、その真なる意味を与え、それを人間の進歩
の度合いに合わせ、適応させるためにやって
来たのです。ですからこの法の中には、教義
の基本である神と隣人に対する私たちの義務
の原則が顕れています。厳密に言うところの
モーセの法では、それらは内容においても、

表現においても、大きく変えられています。
常に外見的な習慣や誤った理解を打ち消そう
としましたが、それらを要約するには、次の
言葉以上に核心的なものとすることはできま
せんでした。「自分を愛するように、神をな
ににも増して愛しなさい」。また、その中に
はすべての法と預言が存在するとつけ加えて
います。「天地が滅び行くまでは、律法の一
点、一画もすたることはなく、ことごとく全
うされるのです」という言葉によって、イエ

スは、神の法が完全に守られること、つまり
、地上においてその法がその純粋さ
を保たれ、すべての方広がりと重要性におい
て実践されることが必要だと述べたかったの
です。しかし、ある種の人間、もしくはある
単一の民族だけの特権を形成するためにその
法が宣言されたのであったとすれば、実際な
人の役に立つことができたでしょうか。神の
子である人類のすべてが、まったく区別され
ることなく、同じように配慮されているので

・外に出て一日でも早く両親の元へ帰えり、親孝行をして、もし、二回目入管に収容をされることがあった時には、母国に帰えりたいと思うこてだと思いますが、帰える前にも、準備帰える前のすることと前から用意をする事で帰えるにはこの準備が必要なものですね。ものごとをするのにはかんでも準備がいると思いますが、帰えるのにも準備ができてないし、お金もないし、チケットもかえないし、帰えるにも帰えれないっていうか帰えかない

判対に家族が日本に誰もいないだったかもっ初めからサインして東京入国管理局から私は帰えっていたと思いますが、その逆で家族は全部全員日本国内にいますから帰えれない。今帰えたらもう二度と両親には会えない気がします。　△△△から日本に来た時には私はまだ小さかったが、おじいちゃんとおばあちゃんが△△△にのこって私がまだ小さい時におじいちゃんとおばあちゃんをなくしました。大好きだったおじいちゃんとおばあちゃ

んには二度と会えなかったからトラウマになっていて今でもまだそのトラウマがあって、それで両親には同じことがおこ、たらどうしようでどうしても考えちゃうんですね。また帰って父と母にもしものことがあるじゃないかと不安と心配です。両親はもう年も年だしいつまでも建康でいおれると思えませんからよけいに考えます。必要以上にも考えます。だから私は帰えらない。例え私がここで死ぬことになっても、死んだから死んだでいいや。

私は人生をかけます。東日本入国管理センターから仮放免で出るか、死んで出るか二つに一つです。入管が出さないであれば死ぬのを待つしかないとちらにせよ、いかっかは必ず出る収容はいつまでも収容も出来ない収容をしたとしても罪のない人間ばかりを収容をしているわけだから法務省の職員みんなそれと入管の職員みんなも最後のしんぱんの時に神も罰をあたえられることをもわすれないでねさばくな、さばかれないためであります。と

人生あきらめたら終わりです。あきらめかいとそう決めたのですが本当に生きて出られるかはわかりません。明日もわかがないと同じように明日は病気になって死んじゃうかもわからかいそれでもう終わりですね。ベトナム人が死んだと同じように入管が大゛んと見ないだから、風邪を引いた時だ、てアスピリンも、もうえないです。おかしい、おかしい。普通風邪薬くらいはもら、てもいいのに入管は何もくれないだからねインフルエンザに、

な、てかかじゃおそいんだよねどうするだよわけわかがないし、何んで薬をくれないだろ本当に病気にな、て時はどうするんだよ入管は、死んでからじゃ遅いしかもう何も出来るわけないじゃん、何で出さないんだろ入管な法務省もなんで外国人を出さないんだろね。普通に考えて出した方がまとまとはらくなのにそれでも出さない大変なほうをわさわさとえらぶし、そして、お金を無駄にしています。本当に国や都道府県などに、国民が納める

お金を無駄にしています。もっと良いことに使えばいいと思います。外国人をどんどん出して無駄にお金を使わないでこれからに来るいろんな出来ごと、じしんなどの自然災害等台風、火事による損失や被害の災難にもっと備えて備えあればうれいなしだかからもっと前もって用意をしておけば心配はいらいです。南海ドラフ地しんが来たか手おくれになる前に私は南海ドラフト地しんは必ずいつ来てもおかしくないと思います。死にたくない.

死ぬもんか。死んでたまるか絶対死なかい死んでも生きるなぜかならばイエス・キリストがおられます。聖書の中にイエス・キリストを信じていればイエス・キリストの名によ、て生きます。命の一番の心配ごとは大きな地しんが来るじゃないかと心配と不安ですね。地しんが来たらこの建物はかんぜんに壊れる違いなく壊れます。古い建物だからかれです。壊れなかたら奇跡だけど、人間の手で使った手は、必ず作った物はみんな壊れます

も頑張っているつもりですが、ここ最近は
部屋に引きこもりみたら北部屋からは出たく
ないし、運動もする気にもなれません。また
元気がない日がふえて来ています。この中に
あと年間いることになるかはわかりませんが
、実際に頭がおかしくなっている人もいます
。俺はそうはなりたいじゃないのけど、長期間
いることだし、いつ出られるかはわからないの
本当に頭がおかしくなるじゃないかと不安で
心配です。早く社会に出してほしいですね。

神経症心配や不安などがもとで、神経のはた
らきがふつうではなくなるゆわれるノイロー
ゼという怖い病気です。頭がおかしくなる前
に一日でも早くここから出たいそれなのです
。一日でも早くアパートた帰って父、母、弟
のそばにいたり親孝行をしたいと考えてます
。家族のそばにいるだけでも私は親孝行だと
思っています。前には何にも出来なかったか
らこそ今現在は、ちゃんと親孝行がしたいの
です。東日本入国管理センターにずーっとい

る今は、親不孝で何も出来ません。だから、
せめて一日でも早く帰えれたらいいなと思う
許可が出るまではまだしばらくの間、何ヵ月
、何年間かはまだわからないけれどもいつか
出られることは、たしかで、ずっと入管を中
にとじこめられるはずがありません。しかし
、2020年までは、入が出るのは少くない
きびしくなると聞いていますから出ることは
出るんだけど、そんなには出られませんね。
私は生きていれば2020年過ぎると思う。

いつかは東日本入国管理センターから両親の
元へ帰えることが本当に夢の中の夢ですね。
いつになるかはわからないけど、ただ夢かも
知れません。本当に出ることが出来たら多分
夢だと思って信じられないかもわかりません
。でも何人も見ていますから、私もいつか同
じように出られたらといつも考えています。
出られないかもわかりませんが、それでも、
頑張るつもりでいます。あきらめたくはない
あきらめたら生きてきた意味もなくなるし、

俺の旅は初めたばかりで道はまだ険しいです、道は果てしなく険しいので、成功するまでの道のりは険しい悪魔からの誘惑良くないことに人をさそいこむからなのです。イエス・キリストを信じていても人間は、しょせん、弱い生き物なので誘惑されればすぐにらくの方をえらぶのが人間です。誰もがらくのほうをえらぶからです。イエス・キリスト信じて悪魔からの誘惑にかてれば何でもうまくいくはずです。ものごとは全部うまく出来ます。

なかなか人間の思うようにはものごとも社会もうまくいかないけど、みながもっと考えて思いを一つに出来れば何でもうまく行きます。日本も、もっと平和にもなります。日本は、最近ちょっと平和じゃなくなった気もする世の中は変わりました。きびしいだけではなくきびしいからさらにきびしいになりました。このままではいけません。東日本入国管理センターの中にいても時々ニュースを見るが、いろんなことが世の中におきていますから

本当にいつイエス・キリストが戻って来てもおかしくないです。刑務所に行た時はイエス・キリストのことも信じていたけど、イエス・キリストを受け入れようと思ったのは本当に今現在、東日本入国管理センターでです。

私もまだまだ覚えなきゃいけないことが山のようにまだまだ沢山有ります。だから聖書の勉強を頑張ろうと思います。しかし、導く人がいないと一人ではとても難しいです。人として進むべき道や、よりよくなるための方法を教えてもらわないとわかりません。もう長期間東日本入国管理センターの中にいるので、精神的にも、ストレスが有る為、精神的なものなので、時々うつ病なのが出て来ます。かるいうつ病とたたかうために

前に進まないといけないって分かっているんだけど前には進めません。法務省や入管などの職員がそうしています。早く許可を出して社会に出せばいいのにと思いますが、物事はそうはうまくいかないみたいだけどいつまでもこうはしていられないのです。入管法務省分かってもらわないといけません。なんで、こうなったのだろうとふしぎでしょうがないなぜ、どうして、いったいなんのためにこうなって

2

いるのかもふしぎでしょうがなりません。もし、イエス・キリストがお戻りになると多くの命は地獄と言って悪いことをした人が死んでから行くとされているところで、キリスト教でも、罪をおかした人が死んでから行くとされているところです。今現在ここがもう地獄のように苦しい思いをしてます。私にとってはここが世界の終わりなのです。

愛する

者よ、悪ことではなく、善いことを見倣ってください。善を行う者は神に属する人であり、悪を行う者は、神を見たことのない人です。イエス・キリストは、みんなに助かってほしいという願いがみんなに同じようになる。一人一人を愛しておられるからなのですね。ここまで分かるようになるにはすごく時間がかかりました。三十年間と言っても良いまた、難しい出来事の日々がありますけれども、イエス・キリストを信じる心が必要なのです。イエス・キリストだけで、少しも混じり気がなければ、純粋な心があれば、キリストを信じさえすればみんなが助けられると思います。悪気はありませんし、みんなには一人でも多くの人に助かってほしいです。キリスト教徒の人はみんなも同じ考えで許し合うこと、互いに許し合うことで、次は、愛と愛の気持ち、自分自身のように隣人を愛しなさいと言って教えています。それから互いに助け合いなさい。とも、言っています。キリスト教は

します。今もイエス・キリストのことを学んでいます。どう学んでいるかというといいうまでもなく基本は、聖書を毎日のように読んでいるけど、中には、難しくてわからないことも多々あります。他にも、イエス・キリストの本や教会のCDを読み聞きをしています。このくりかえしをしながら毎日新しいことを学んでいます。毎日読むことによって私は、成長していっています。毎日聖書読むことにより毎日聖書は、違う御言葉かのように私に

話しかけてくれるのです。私は特別な人ではないが、普通の人にはわからない多分読んでも、うん、で、終わちゃうことぐらいも分かります。あるいは、話しをしても、普通の人は、うんって言って終わるかのどっちかですね。多くの人は、ことわりますが、中には、前の私みたいに無神論者だった時期があったあの時みたいな感じでみんなは神を信じない人も多くいます。私の知り合いにも何人も、います。でもなんとかして神の御言葉伝える

新約聖書のマタイによる福音書を読みました。同じく、マルコによる福音書を読みました。同じく、ルカによる福音書を読みました。新約聖書のヨハネによる福音書も読みました。四つの福音書くりかえし読んだことです。何回読んだかはわかりません。何回も何回も数え切れないほど読んだと思います。しかし、今でもわからないことやちょっとぎもんに思うこともあります。もし、全部はじめから分かるだったらこんなにも読む必要がないと

も思ったことやはじめから分かっていればと後悔こうがいする日もありましたが、だけど戻ることは出来ませんのであと戻り出来ません。時をまきもどせたらいいのにって思う時だってありました。でも、そんな簡単には物事はうまくいくはずがないし、もう前にすすむしかないのです。しっぱいしながらでも前にすすまないとけして前にはすすめません。今現在東日本入国管理センターにいるけど進めないのと、帰るにも帰えれないだから今

仮放免が許可になるまで待つ以外ありません。私がビザがあった頃は、ボランティア活動をやったことがあります。はじめてやったは、体などが不自由な子供達に面会をしました。あとは、ホームレスの人達に弁当を届けたり、昔、お金をあげたりもしました。あとは、町のゴミ拾いと最後には、まだ二十歳にはなっていなかったので、未成年の時でした。二十歳になって成人式をやって無事に終えてハローワークに通いはじめてからパン屋さんに就職しましたが、夜遊びしていたために、長続きしませんでした。また、ハローワーク人通いでは、工場で自動車の部品の製造加工の就職やホテル内で、ないむという就職にもつきましたし、力仕事のとび、どかた、建設作業員、解体作業もやりました。アルバイトやったりして、真面目に過ごしたこともあった時期もありました。どれも長続きしなかったこうして2年間、22歳まではなんとかやっていたのですが、残念ながら警察に浦りました

捕→

他には、浅念なことにものごとをは、きりとさせるためのもとになるものはありませんが、あとは、人を自殺から救ったり、いじめにあっていた友達を助けたり、けんかを止めたり、友人や知人のけんかにまで間にはいってあげて止めたりもしました。これらのことによって多くの人や方々が救くわれたと思う。しょうめいするものがないからしょうがないんだけど、入管にわからなくても自分自身と神だけが分かります。私は、イエスキリストとともに居て、イエス・キリストと私とともに居れば良いと思い考えています。それから家族、父、母、弟の三人だけですが、私には十分かもわかりません。いつか自分の家族も作って家族がいっしょに生活が出来る場所で、日本だろうと△△△だろうとも神に全てゆだねます。仮放免では、結婚は難しいので、他の人に任せるよりも神にその場の状況を任せたいと考えています。神も私の考えごとがごぞんじのことだと思うので任せることに

残

僕はまだ未熟者ですが、今は只々仮放免で、社会に出て被害者の方々にごめんなさいと、言いたいのでちゃんと謝罪して迷惑をかけたことを謝罪したいと与えてますがいつかはここから無事に出られることしか考えません。ちゃんと認められていつか出られることを信じてます。父なる神様は生きている神様、だから神様を信じていればいつか奇跡をおこすかもわかりません。なぜならば自分は、死にかけたことが何回もありました。神は、この自分を何ども救ってくださったのです。今があるのは神様のおかげと言、てもいい神様がいなかったら自分もこの世にはいないと考えていましてつくずく思います。だから時間を無駄にしないで信仰をもって強めて行きたいとも考えてます。簡単なことではないが、不可能じゃないのです。

東日本入国管理センターの中で、日本語勉強や聖書の勉強も、もちろんのことやってます。家族がこられないので、家族のサポートとボランティアの方々のサポートがあります。家族にも来てもらいたいけど仕方ありません。その変りに神は、ボランティアの方々から御言葉を伝える為にわざわざ私やほかの人のためにも来てくださいます。面会がここで一週間の中で平日は一番の楽しみにしてます。みんなはどうか知らないけど私は本当に、一番の楽しみは来てくださるボランティアの方々なのです。別に物をもらいたくてここに来てほしいわけではありません。神の御言葉を聞きたくて毎週楽しみに待っていますね。こないこともありますけど、次の週まで待、ているとボランティアの方が一人は来ます。一週間ない時はさびしいですよ。でも次の週に来ていただくとうれしい気持ちでさびしさを忘れてしまいます。いつまでもこのままじゃいけないと自覚しています仕方ありませんまと数カ月で二年間の長期間収容されてますす。もうトタールで九年間社会には出ていない、いつか頭がおかしくなってノイローゼなるじゃないかと思われます。入管も法務省などの人達がぜんぜん社会に出さないからです。自分は一際責任は取りません。もうどうなってても自分は知らないただ仮放免で社会へと出してほしいし、自由がほしいのだから自分は、仮放免になってもかまいませんだから、仮放免が許可になるまでは頑張るつもりです

。命あるかぎりは、最後までに例え死んでも△△△　には帰えりたくないのです。しかし、無理矢というやっかいな制度がありまして、法務省や法務大臣かつめいれいがあると、入管は、それにしたがう然えざるおえません。その時はもう人生は終わりなのです。またチャンスがあれば自分は、真面目に学校に、行きたいという夢が今だにありますだから、高校に行けるようにしたいと思います。でもまだどうなるかは誰にも分かからないのです。

私はキリスト教徒で実は東日本入国管理ここで当センターにいながら今現在キリスト受け入れようと思いました。いつかここから出られたら洗礼を受けようと思います。ですからここから生きて出られることをお祈りしてますが、なかなか出られそうにありませんから凹むこともありますが、そんな時こそイエスキリストを信じて必ず力をくださるのだから今はなんとかやってこられてきてますので、多分大丈夫だと思います。手紙まくれになか

なければ良いのですが、やはり心配ですね。ここ最近は、自然災害の災難台風、地しん、火事、大雨の豪雨などによる損失や被害です。これら全部イエス・キリストがいつ戻って来てもおかしくないというサインのはじまりで、いつ戻って来るかは誰にもわからないの。神にだけしかわかりません。みなが一人一人目を覚めるためであります。そのためにも、誤りやわるかったことに気づいて直す必要があります。そうすれば、みなが助かります。

法律に厳格とわかってりました。だから自分は、ちゃんと法令を守っていると思っていましたが今回のことで、意識が足りなかったと分かりました。本当にすみませんでした。ごめんなさい、ごめんなさい。自分の不注意で当局に多大なご迷惑をおかけしました。本当に申し訳ありませんでした。今後はこのようなことのないよう約束します。したがいまして、仮放免許可をいただきましても、自分の法令遵守及び出頭確保になな支違はありませ

ん。仮放免を許可いただきますようお願い申し上げます。自分は日本の法律は絶対に守ると約束するし、入国管理局の指示は全て守ると約束します。一番初めに東京入国管理局に書いた理由ですけど、私は東京入国管理局に来てもう早いもので三ヵ月以上になりました。入管た入ってから三ヵ月になってしまいました。でもまだはじまりにすぎません。私のやった行動を良く考えています。その行動が日本の法律を違反して間違えました。周囲に

迷惑をかける責任の重い行動であることも、痛感じましたから深く反省しています。未来でもう二度と絶対にしません。絶対にしません。もうしないです。今後はもう二度と絶対にしません。今の希望を抱いているのが、日本の農業的と日本語を学ぶことの夢かんです。そのことを実現する為た仮放免許可を認めうれる望んでいます。ここに毎日一日一日一生懸命勉強して頑張っています。規則をちゃんと守って真面目生きますから解放しても

、されても問題はありません。本当に心から機会をいただきたいです。どうぞ宜しくお願い申し上げます。

△△△

と書きましたが、残念ながら一回目は、ダメというきびしいけっかでした。二回目もダメ三回目もダメ四回目もダメそれから五回目も不許可というきびしいけっかの数々なのです。絶対におかしいし、何んで、どうしてだ、なぜ、何のためにとやりようがありません。どうしたら認められるようになるのでしょう

一長期間収用されている。仮放免のけっかが
長引く為、弁護士にいらいしても仮放免が、
不許可になっても理由がわからないし、けっ
かがおそい、もっと早く教えてほしいです。
長期間収用されても一年以内で、精神的問題
や家族のけつえんの問題がいけつがあります
。二、痛み止めしか出さないし、ちゃんとし
たちりょうやってないので病気になります
。しょうじょうを言ってもようすう見るしか
言わない。ちゃんとしたちりょうもやってい

ほしい薬の意味がない病院もつれてもらえな
いし、薬の服用しても何をのまされているか
わからないので、薬読んでいても、読んでい
る最中もうつびょうになったり、ふうみん症
食良くふしんになっている方々が何人もいる
三、不衛生収容されていることでちゃんとし
てほしいことの意見も多くあります。そして
衛生等については、入管が毎日ちゃんとなが
きれいにすることを法律の本になりますかか
法律をちゃんと守ってください。

△△△

長生きをしたいため薬をやめしたしたけど、
一つだけ読んでいる薬があります。高血圧の
薬です。血圧が平均の数値よりかなり高かっ
たので、脳卒中や心臓病などの原因になる。
中には、低血圧の人もいます。どっちらも、
危ない病気の一類です。東日本入国管理に
収容されて長期収容だし、毎日薬を読んでい
るし、毎日毎日薬を読んでいてとても心配で
薬の長期にもらう服用はけして体にとって良
くないのでとても心配でなりません。また

精神的にも追い詰められています。体には、
けして良くない。自分自身はもうそろそろ二
年以上で、成長したと思っています。毎日の
ように自分の行動や人生を見つめることが
出来ました。そして今後日本で生活していく
ためにも、もっと日本語を覚える日本語の独
習するし、日本語文法書（名詞、動詞
、助詞）漢字をも学んでいるし、読み書きも
出来ます。わからない言葉があると辞書で調
べます。自分は日本で生活していて日本は、

このままではダメです。長期間になったため
「もう出してもらわなきゃ」家族も待ってくれ
ているし」いつまでも待っていることはない
いつか家族だって旅び立つことがおそろしい
自分自身もいつまでもつかはわかりません。
入管はちょっとずつ命を奪っていってます。
本当は長く生きたいけど、入管の中にいては
長生き出来そうにありません。早死になると
思います。入管の中では、日々のストレスや
つかれがたまりにたまって頭がおかしくなる

じゃないかと不安でなりません。本当に心配
で時にはカウンセリングも受けることなども
ありました。最近はやめたけど、仮放免ダメ
って言われるたんびに残念な気持ちだけ
ではなく悲しみなどの気持ちが出てきます。
今現在は健康だけど、いつまでも健康でいか
れません。風邪を引いた時は入管は風邪の薬
でさえくれません。このままだと本当に大変
なことになります。もう若くないので病気が
心配になって来ます。一日でも早く帰りたい

第五十四条第二項には、入国者収容所長又は
主任審査官は、前項の請求により、又は職権で
、法務省令で定めるところにより、収容令書
又は退去強制令書の発付を受けて収容されて
いる者の情状及び仮放免の請求の理由となる
証拠並びにその者の性格、資産等を考慮して
、三百万円を超えない範囲内で法務省令で定
める額の保証金を納付させ、かつ、住居及び
行動範囲の制限、呼出しに対する義務その他
必要と認める条件を付して、その者を仮放免

することができる。」となりますが、入管は
この法律を守っていないし、法務省も同じく
ぜんぜん法律を守ってません。仮放免おそい
第一に仮放免のけっかがおそすぎます。また
第二に保証金が高いのでもっと下てほしい。
第三に外や刑務所の人全々仮放免で出てない
第四に薬を出してもらえなかったりなどです
第五に不衛生なところが数多く見かれます。
第六に病院にはつれてってもらえないなど。
第七になんでもたいようが遅いのです。意見

自首して転機訪れました。「それでも目の前が真っ暗になりました。ところが、このお先真っ暗な逮捕が本当は救いだったんですね。何が救いなのかは、人間にはわかりません。なぜなら僕の再生の人生は、この逮捕から始まったのだから、今回警察にパクられてからすでにスタートしていたことに最近思います。今現在も、逮捕されて良かったと思います。古約聖書のエゼキエル書33章11節こうある私は悪人が死ぬのを喜ばない。かえってその悪人が態度を悔い改めて、生き直す事を私は喜ぶ。立ち返れ、立ち返れ、お前の悪しき道から。

△△△よ、どうしておまえが死んで良いのだろうか。ここから、これから、悔い改めて、厚生して、反省して

△△△という人間は、新しい人間を目差しますよ。そして、弱い人間を守れる強い人間になる。今の希望があるとすれば高校に行って高校を取りたいと思います。今現在の夢もいつか、大学に行くことです。神学校に行きたいです

人の命を何よりも尊重してます。ですから、人間が生まれながらにもっている、自由や平等などの権利がある自由になるべきである。ちゃんと人権を守ってほしいものであるべき外に出したくないからって言って入管をして法務省が人をある場所に閉じこめて、外に出られないようにしてます。法律を守っているだけと言いながら入管と法務省は罪をおかしています。その罪は犯罪です。罪もない人間を閉じこめているからなのです。

△△△

や他の人間をも監禁してます。盗み罪です。入管は人間の命を奪っています。罪もない人の命まで奪っています。死んだベトナム人やインド人がいい例です。仮放免社会の中で決められているしくみや決まり、ちゃんと仮放免制度があるにもかかわらず出さない。入管がぜんぜん出さない。普通じゃないからおかしい筋道物事の正しいわけになってないことばかり普通仮放免制度があるのならば、社会へ帰えすのが筋ではないのでしょうか。

T's Voice (T's Own Writing)

十歳で　△△△から日本に初めてきました。
小学校は真面目な小学生だった中学校から、
ちょっとやんちゃな中学生で無免許で警察に
捕まりました。鑑別と少年院や特別少年院も
入り、刑務所も初めてで最後の刑務所生活
おくりました。刑務所7年間の事件だったん
だけど、頑張って6年2ヵ月で10ヵ月早く外
に出られるかと思えば残念ながら外には出れ
ずにそのまま入管につれていかれましたので
、それからもう2年になろうとしています。

東京入国管理局から東日本入国管理センター
という過酷な試練の中生活をして頑張ってい
ますが、入管はぜんぜん出さないこれまでは
5回も仮放免申請の手続きをしていますが、
社会に帰れそうにもありません。一日でも、
早く両親の元へ帰えりたい気持ちなんだけど
ここから出られません。出られても仕事出来
ません。学歴「歴」もない人間になってしま
い人生の悲しみのどん底まで落ちました。一
番つらいことは家族に会えないことですね。

〈著者紹介〉

田巻 松雄 (たまき・まつお)

宇都宮大学国際学部教授。国際学部附属多文化公共圏センターが運営するHANDS事業(外国人児童生徒の教育支援事業)代表。社会学博士。主な研究テーマは、日本におけるホームレス問題、東アジアにおける国際的な人の移動、外国人児童生徒の教育問題。2021年9月から栃木県宇都宮市に、主に義務教育を十分に受けることが出来なかった人や日本語が不自由な外国人が学ぶことが出来る自主夜間中学を開始する。

【英文版】宇都宮大学国際学叢書第12巻

ある外国人の日本での20年
—外国人児童生徒から「不法滞在者」へ

From Foreign Child to Illegal Immigrant:
The Case of T, a Brazilian Man of Japanese Descent
Who Lived in Japan for 20 Years

2021年8月31日　初版　第1刷発行

著　者：田巻 松雄
発行所：下野新聞社
〒320-8686 宇都宮市昭和1-8-11
電話028-625-1135
https://www.shimotsuke.co.jp
印　刷：シナノパブリッシングプレス
装　丁：デザインジェム　橋本 剛

Printed in Japan
ISBN978-4-88286-796-8 C3036